# THE GLASS MENAGERIE and A STREETCAR NAMED DESIRE

# NOTES

*including*

- *Scene Summaries and Commentaries*
- *Character Sketches*
- *Selected Questions*
- *Suggested Theme Topics*
- *Selected Bibliography*

*by*
*James L. Roberts, Ph.D.*
*Department of English*
*University of Nebraska*

Wiley Publishing, Inc.

*Editor*
Gary Carey, M.A., University of Colorado

*Consulting Editor*
James L. Roberts, Ph.D., Department of English, University of Nebraska

*Composition*
Wiley Indianapolis Composition Services

**CliffsNotes™ *The Glass Menagerie & A Streetcar Named Desire***

Published by:
Wiley Publishing, Inc.
111 River Street
Hoboken, NJ 07030
www.wiley.com




ISBN: 0-8220-0533-6

20 19 18 17 16 15 14 13 12 11
1O/TR/QX/QW/IN
Published by Wiley Publishing, Inc., New York, NY
Published simultaneously in Canada


For general information on our other products and services or to obtain technical support, please contact our Customer Care Department within the U.S. at 800-762-2974, outside the U.S. at 317-572-3993, or fax 317-572-4002.

Wiley also publishes its books in a variety of electronic formats. Some content that appears in print may not be available in electronic books.

# CONTENTS

## AUTHOR'S LIFE AND BACKGROUND

More than with most authors, Tennessee Williams' personal life and experiences have been the direct subject matter for his dramas. He uses his experiences so as to universalize them through the means of the stage. Thus, his life is utilized over and over again in the creation of his dramas.

Tennessee Williams was born Thomas Lanier Williams in Columbus, Mississippi. Because his father was a traveling salesman and was often away from home, he lived the first ten years of his life in his maternal grandparents' home. His father was a loud, outgoing, hard drinking, boisterous man who bordered on the vulgar, at least as far as the young sensitive Tennessee Williams was concerned. In contrast to his father, his mother seemed to be rather quiet and possessive, demonstrating a tremendous attachment to her children. Tennessee was himself a rather delicate child who was plagued with several serious childhood diseases which kept him from attending regular school. Instead, he read profusely in his grandfather's library.

His maternal grandfather was an Episcopal rector, apparently a rather liberal and progressive individual. Even though there are several portraits of the clergy in Williams' later works, none seemed to be built on the personality of his real grandfather.

Perhaps because his early life was spent in an atmosphere of genteel culture, the greatest shock to Williams was the move his family made when he was about twelve. The father accepted a position in a shoe factory in St. Louis and moved the family from the expansive Episcopal home in the South to an ugly tenement building in St. Louis. Their cramped apartment and the ugliness of the city life seemed to make a lasting impression on the boy. Here in school he was often ridiculed for his southern accent, and he was never able to find acceptance. Likewise, his father who had been a traveling salesman, was suddenly at home most of the time.

It was here in St. Louis that Williams' slightly older sister, Rose, began to cease to develop as a person and failed to cross over the barrier from childhood to adulthood. She, like Laura in *The Glass Menagerie*, began to live in her own world of glass ornaments. Eventually, she had to be placed in an institution. She became the model for Laura Wingfield. The description of Laura's room, just across the alley from the Paradise Dance Club, is also a description of his sister's room. Laura's desire to lose herself from the world was a characteristic of his own sister. And both were seen by Williams as being shy, quiet, but lovely girls who were not able to cope with the modern world.

After Tennessee finished high school, he went to the University of Missouri for three years until he failed ROTC. At the university he began to write more and discovered alcohol as a cure for his over-sensitive shyness. After his third year, his father got him a position in the shoe factory. He worked there for two years; he later classified this time as the most miserable two years of his life. He spent dreary days at the warehouse and then devoted his nights to writing poetry, plays, and short stories. After two years of working all day and writing all night, he had a nervous breakdown and went to Memphis, Tennessee, to recuperate with his grandfather who had moved there after retirement. His years of frustration and his dislike of the warehouse job are reflected directly in the character of Tom Wingfield who followed essentially the same pattern that Williams himself followed. In fact, Tennessee gave this character his own first name, Tom.

During all of this time, Tennessee had been winning small prizes for various types of writing, but nothing significant had yet been written. After his rest in Memphis, he returned to the university (Washington University in St. Louis), where he became associated with a writers' group. Here he wrote and had some of his earlier works produced. He later attended the State University of Iowa and wrote two long plays for a creative writing seminar. After leaving Iowa, he drifted around the country, picking up odd jobs and collecting experiences until he received a Rockefeller Fellowship in 1940. He spent his time writing until the money was exhausted and then he worked again at odd jobs until his first great success with *The Glass Menagerie* in 1944-45. Since then, Williams has produced one success after another.

Williams has used his early life in most of his plays. His favorite setting is southern, with southern characters. In Stanley Kowalski, we see many of the rough, poker-playing, manly qualities that his own father possessed. In Laura and Amanda, we find very close echoes to his own mother and sister. In Tom Wingfield, we find again the struggles and aspirations of the writer himself re-echoed in literary form. Thus he has objectified his own subjective experiences in his literary works.

Tennessee Williams' plays are still controversial. There are many critics who call him sensational and shocking, but his plays have attracted the widest audience of any living American dramatist, and he is established as America's most important dramatist.

# THE GLASS MENAGERIE

*by Tennessee Williams*

## PLOT SUMMARY

In the Wingfield apartment in St. Louis, the mother, Amanda, lives with her crippled daughter and her working son, Tom. At dinner she tells her daughter, Laura, to stay nice and pretty for her gentlemen callers even though Laura has never had any callers and expects none. Amanda remembers the time that she had seventeen gentlemen callers all on one Sunday afternoon. Amanda then tells Laura to practice her shorthand and typing. A few days later Amanda comes home from Laura's school after finding out that Laura had dropped out several months earlier. Amanda is shocked and wonders what they will do with their lives since Laura refuses to try to help and spends all her time playing with her glass menagerie and her old phonograph records. Amanda decides that they must have a gentleman caller for Laura, and Laura tells her that she has liked only one boy in her whole life, a high school boy named Jim.

When Tom goes out to the movies that night, Amanda accuses him of doing something else rather than going to the movies every night. They have an argument, and the next morning after Tom apologizes, Amanda asks him to find some nice gentleman caller for Laura and to bring him home for dinner. A few days later, Tom tells Amanda that he has invited a young man named Jim O'Connor home for dinner. Amanda immediately begins to make rather elaborate plans for the gentleman caller.

On the next night, Amanda oversees Laura's dress and adds some "gay deceivers" to the dress to make Laura more attractive. When she mentions the name of the gentleman caller, Laura realizes that it is possibly the same Jim on whom she had a crush in high school. She tells her mother that she might not be able to come for dinner if it is the same one. Amanda will have nothing to do with such foolishness, and even though Laura is sick when the gentleman caller arrives, Amanda forces her to open the door. And it is the Jim that she knew from high school. At dinner she is physically sick and has to be excused.

Later, Amanda sends Jim, the gentleman caller, into the living room to keep Laura company while she and Tom do the dishes. As Jim and Laura talk, she loses some of her shyness and becomes rather charming. Jim is attracted by Laura's quiet charms, but later after having kissed her, he must explain that he is already engaged. When Amanda re-appears, Jim explains to her also that he is engaged and must go. Amanda is so stunned that she accuses Tom of deliberately playing a trick on them. The play ends with Tom some years in the future thinking back on his sister Laura whom he can never forget.

## CHARACTERS

### *Amanda Wingfield*

The mother whose husband deserted her years ago leaving her with a son and daughter to raise. She lives partially in the world of her youth and her gentlemen callers in order to escape the brutalities of today's world.

*Tom Wingfield*

Her son who is employed in a shoe warehouse in order to support the family. He is a poet by nature and feels that his environment is destroying his creative abilities.

*Laura Wingfield*

The daughter who is slightly crippled. She has retreated from this world and lives in a world of old phonograph records and little glass animals.

*Jim O'Connor*

The "emissary" from the world of reality. He is the average or ordinary young man who brings a touch of the common world into the Wingfield world of dreams.

## STRUCTURE THROUGH MEMORY

The structure of the play involves the presentation of the scenes through the memory of one of the characters. Tom Wingfield is both the narrator and a character in the play. The separate scenes, then, should be seen as part of Tom's memory of a crucial time in his life. The scenes do not function to give us a traditional plot or story-line, but instead, they are selected to give the audience a slice of life that the author once lived through. In his own world, he wants to present truth through illusion; that is, he wants to try to say something about his life by recalling certain scenes of his past life. Thus the play is structured upon the principle of presenting a series of episodes which should accumulate to make a total comment about a specific life.

This type of structure forces Tom to be both a narrator and a character in the play. He must let the audience know that these are scenes from memory and that he is both the person remembering them and the person centrally involved in the scenes. Some critics have objected to this structure because, as they point out, Tom could not possibly know what happened in the scene between Laura and the gentleman caller. But as Tom suggests, he takes the license of a poet and projects himself into scenes in order to present poetic truths.

The stage directions call for the use of several technical devices in order to convey the idea that this is a memory play. For example, some of the scenes should be presented with some type of net or gauze between the audience and the actors. Or in many places, Williams suggests the use of titles and images to be projected on a scene in order to force or reinforce the idea of memory and to recall certain events that occurred during the time of the play. Others are supposed to be used to suggest some symbolic aspect of the play. But when the play is produced, they are virtually never used. Most directors feel that the play is sufficient without the extra use of images. In fact, most directors feel that the use of these images would detract from the central action of the play. But the point is that Williams included them so as to help with the structure of the play as a memory play.

## SCENE SUMMARIES & COMMENTARIES

### SCENE ONE

*Summary*

At the rise of the curtain, we see an old-fashioned tenement apartment. We can also see the narrow alleyways which surround the apartment. Tom Wingfield, the narrator, enters and addresses the audience. Tom explains that the play is a memory play and that he is one of the characters in the play. The other characters are his mother Amanda, his sister Laura, and a gentleman caller. There is another character who never appears. This is his father who deserted the family some long years ago—"He was a telephone man who fell in love with long distances!"

As the action begins, Amanda is instructing Tom about how to eat every bite of his food until Tom yells at her that he can't enjoy a bite of his food because of her constant nagging. Amanda then tells Laura to stay fresh and pretty for the gentlemen callers. Laura tells her she isn't expecting any, and Amanda tells how one Sunday afternoon in Blue Mountain, Mississippi, she had seventeen gentlemen callers all on one afternoon. Tom and Laura have heard this story many times but listen patiently to it again. Amanda then sends Laura into the living room to practice her shorthand or typing and to stay pretty for the gentlemen callers in spite of Laura's reassertion that there will be none.

*Commentary*

A.

The fire escape, a physical symbol, is used symbolically to represent various aspects of being trapped or as a method of escape. As Williams writes, the "huge buildings are always burning with the slow and implacable fires of human desperation." The play then presents Tom's frustrated attempt to escape from his intolerable job, situation, and life. For Amanda, the escape is seen in terms of the gentleman caller who will rescue her daughter from potential old-maidhood. But then, for Laura the escape is seen as her means of retreating (or escaping) from the outer world. It is her protection from this outside world—a world which stares at her deformity. In other words, whereas for Tom, it is an escape *to* the outer world, for Laura it is an escape *from* an outer world which she dreads so much. This will be symbolically portrayed later in the play when Amanda forces Laura to go to the store and Laura trips on the fire escape, symbolizing her dread of the hostile outside world.

B.

Use of the Narrator: The technique of using a narrator is often considered a trick by the artist so that he will not have to conceive of imaginative ways to convey exposition—that is, ways of communicating background information necessary to the present understanding of the play. (For example, a traditional technique, used by Henrik Ibsen, was to have two servants—one newly hired and one regular—on stage talking about their master and, in this way, the audience learned all that was necessary in order to understand the present action.)

The use of Tom, however, is integrated into the play. He presents the play as a memory and then steps back into time to become one of the participants in the action.

C.

In his opening monologue, Tom says that the stage magician "gives you illusion that has the appearance of truth. I give you truth in the pleasant disguise of illusion." Here he means that the regular dramatist creates a dramatic illusion on the stage which the audience takes for the truth. But this play, by its techniques, offers itself as illusion, but Williams maintains that it is actually truth disguised as illusion. Thus, the meaning of his later statement that the play is not realistic, is that the play is being presented through the memory of Tom.

D.

The essence of Amanda's character is caught in her first speech. She seems to need to nag at her children, especially Tom, and she is not even aware that she is nagging. Essentially, she must have something to talk about, and she nags at Tom about little things because she fears that she has lost or is losing him as far as the big things, the significant things, in life are concerned.

E.

Amanda's sense of unreality is caught in these first episodes as she lives in a world of servants and gentlemen callers. Always her language suggests another time and place.

F.

Note that all of Amanda's so-called gentlemen callers either came from the wealthy or became wealthy. The question will arise as to whether she actually had these callers or not. Amanda might have been somewhat popular, but it is almost inconceivable to believe that she actually did have as many as seventeen gentlemen callers. But what is important is that Amanda now believes this story so strongly that the gentlemen callers have become a reality for her.

G.

The scene ends again on Amanda's return to the subject of Laura's gentlemen callers. She closes her mind to the reality that Laura has no gentlemen callers. The question here is whether Amanda wants the callers for Laura or whether she wants them so as to relive her own youth. It seems in this scene that Amanda is thinking only of herself, but later we will see that she is afraid of what will happen to a young girl of Laura's position who is not married. Thus, Amanda's emotions are mixed at present but will become clearer as the play progresses.

H.

Even though this is a short scene, note that the author has carefully filled it with most of the essential meanings of the entire play. The nagging, the gentleman caller, Tom's restlessness, and Laura's shyness are all presented in this first scene. Even the fact that Amanda tells Laura to practice her shorthand or to study the typing chart prepares the reader for the beginning of the next scene where Amanda discovers Laura's deception about her failure in school.

## SCENE TWO

*Summary*

Laura is sitting alone playing with her glass collection. When she hears Amanda ascending the stairs, she immediately hides the collection and sits before the typing chart pretending to study it. Amanda comes in and theatrically drops her gloves on the floor. When Laura asks her what is wrong, Amanda accuses her of deception. Amanda tells Laura that she was by the business school in order to inquire about Laura's progress. It was then that she found out that Laura had not been attending school. Amanda is depressed about losing the fifty dollars tuition and about Laura's future. Laura explains that on the day she was supposed to take her first speed test in typing, she became sick and threw up on the floor. Since then she has been pretending to go to school, but instead she has been going to the museums and to the bird houses in the zoo and to a big glass house where they "raise the tropical flowers."

Amanda wonders what will then happen to a girl who can't work and who has no gentlemen callers. She then wonders if Laura has ever liked a boy. Laura tells about a boy in high school named Jim with whom she was infatuated. He used to call her "blue roses" because she had had pleurosis which he thought sounded like blue roses. Amanda then decides that Laura must get married. Laura protests that she is a cripple, but Amanda refuses to allow Laura to use that word and insists that all Laura needs to do is to develop charm.

*Commentary*

A.

In the first episode, Amanda had told Laura to go practice her shorthand. At the opening of this scene, we see that Laura rapidly hides her glass ornaments and acts as though she is practicing her typing when she hears Amanda ascending the fire escape. This scene, then, handles the revelation that Laura has not been going to her school.

B.

This revelation has tremendous import for Amanda. First it represents a fifty dollar loss of the tuition money—money which was very hard to come by. But more important, it forces Amanda to consider the future and to face, realistically, problems that she does not like to think about—that is, that she has a daughter who is crippled and who is too sensitive to work. These thoughts, in turn, bring to Amanda's mind the need for a gentleman caller.

C.

Thus we see a relationship between the gentleman caller and Laura's ineptitude in any type of work. Amanda sums up Laura's position by saying: "I know so well what becomes of unmarried women who aren't prepared to occupy a position. I've seen such pitiful cases in the South—barely tolerated spinsters living upon the grudging patronage of sister's husband or brother's wife...encouraged by one in-law to visit another." Of course what Amanda did not say was that her knowledge is first hand because she became one of those pitiful cases who was not prepared to occupy a position. Thus with Laura's inability to occupy a position, it becomes urgent to find her a husband so that she doesn't become one of those pitiful creatures.

D.

Note how Amanda plays the revelation scene for all its theatrical effect. This is also a part of her character and prepares us for her giddy actions when the gentleman caller comes.

E.

This scene also prepares us for the coming of Jim, the gentleman caller, because he was a high school friend of both Tom and Laura. With it now established that he was Laura's high school idol, we are more prepared to accept her nervousness when he arrives.

F.

Even though a few minutes earlier Amanda was able to face reality enough to discuss what happens to unmarried women, now with the thought of a gentleman caller coming, she suddenly resorts back to a world of illusion and refuses to allow Laura to refer to herself as crippled. She then tells Laura to develop *charm* to compensate for her slight defect. For Laura to develop charm is totally impossible, and furthermore, the type of charm that Amanda means would destroy what innocent appeal Laura now possesses.

## SCENE THREE

### *Summary*

Tom explains how his mother, once she had decided that a gentleman caller was necessary, set all her energy to preparing for one. She began a campaign on the telephone to recruit subscribers for a popular woman's magazine.

When the scene opens, Tom and his mother are arguing about a book by D. H. Lawrence that she took back to the library because she refuses to have such a hideous book in her house. Tom reminds her that he pays the rent on the house. Tom then prepares to leave to go to the movies. Amanda screams at him that he can't stay out late at night and still do a good day's work. Tom reminds her how much he hates his job at the warehouse. When Amanda accuses Tom of doing something he is ashamed of every night and accuses him of lying about going every night to the movies, Tom becomes infuriated and tells his mother a fantastic tale and ends by calling her an "ugly – babbling – witch." Tom tries to get his coat on and in his rapid struggle to leave, he throws his coat against the wall and shatters Laura's glass menagerie.

*Commentary*

A.

One of Amanda's admirable qualities is her determination. Once she has set her mind to a task, she goes about it with a determination that neither of her children possesses. It would be impossible to imagine either Tom or Laura dedicating themselves to a task with such complete zeal as does Amanda.

B.

It is, however, this dedication which makes her appear hateful to her children. It is as though both, especially Tom, were still youths whose every action had to be supervised.

C.

When the quarrel began, Tom was apparently in the midst of trying to write something creative when Amanda interrupted him. The violence of the quarrel has other implications. Besides the nagging, the responsibility and the gloomy life, Tom's privacy has been intruded upon, here represented by the fact that Amanda has carried his book by Lawrence back to the library. Thus if Amanda is the type to look upon the novels of D. H. Lawrence as "filth," then there is little chance for Tom to find understanding and sympathy for his own creative efforts.

D.

During the quarrel, we find out that Tom hates his job at the warehouse and furthermore goes every night to the movies in order to find some type of escape. Like Tennessee Williams, Tom thinks of the warehouse job as destructive to the creative endeavors of man.

E.

At the end of the scene, Tom's violent action causes some of Laura's glass to be shattered. Tom returns to pick up the glass but is unable to utter a word. This symbolically represents Laura's inner feelings. During the scene she has had nothing to say, but the lighting is always focused on her, because during scenes such as these, it is Laura who suffers the most, and she must sense that much of the antagonism between Tom and Amanda stems from her position. That is, Laura must know that she is an extra burden on Tom and that he feels this responsibility for her. And she knows that Amanda constantly worries about her. Thus, the shattered glass seems to represent Laura's shattered inner feelings. In the next scene, she will attempt to reconcile Tom and Amanda.

## SCENE FOUR

*Summary*

At the beginning of the scene, Tom is just returning from the movies. He explains to Laura, who is awake, that the movie was very long, and there was a magician who could perform tricks such as escaping from a coffin which had been nailed shut. The scene fades out and comes in again with Amanda calling for Tom to "rise and shine!" Laura asks Tom to apologize to Amanda for their argument of the preceding evening. Amanda sends Laura to the store for butter and tells her to charge it even though Laura has qualms about charging anything else. As Laura leaves, she trips on the fire escape and Tom rushes to help her. After she is gone, Tom slowly and reluctantly apologizes to Amanda. Then almost immediately, Amanda begins to tell Tom how and what to eat for his breakfast. But mainly, she wants to talk about Laura. Amanda feels that Laura broods about Tom's unhappiness. She then inquires as to why Tom goes so often to the movies. Tom explains that he likes adventure. Amanda maintains that a man finds adventure in his work or else he does without it. When Tom attempts to explain that man is by instinct a lover, hunter, etc., Amanda recoils and will not listen to talk about instinct.

Amanda tells Tom that they must be making plans for Laura. She has seen the letter that Tom has received from the Merchant Marine and knows that he is planning to leave them, but she tells Tom that he must first see to it that Laura is provided for, because Laura can't spend her life playing old phonograph records and fooling with "those pieces of glass." Amanda then asks Tom to see if he can find some nice young man at the warehouse and bring him home for dinner in order to meet Laura. Tom promises to try to find someone and immediately Amanda renews her campaign to get more subscribers for her magazine.

*Commentary*

A.

When Tom returns from the movies, he emphasizes his desire to escape by talking about the magician who was nailed in a coffin and got out. He then compares his apartment and his situation in life to that of the magician climbing into a coffin – now the question is how he can get out of *his* coffin.

B.

Notice that Laura trips on the outside fire escape, a device used to suggest her fear of the outside world.

C.

As soon as Tom apologizes to his mother, she maintains theatrically that her devotion has made her a witch and hateful to her children. There is a great deal of truth in this statement. Her overzealous devotion causes her to nag and almost persecute them.

D.

The quarrel has hardly cooled off before Amanda returns to her old nagging self. She immediately begins to direct Tom as to how he should drink his coffee and what he should eat.

E.

The difference between Amanda and Tom is most clearly seen in this scene in their discussion of *instinct*. Tom is the poet and feels that man should live by his feelings and by his instinct. He feels that he is being destroyed as an individual by being forced to live all cramped up in the apartment and in the city. He seeks love, adventure, and romance. But these are the very qualities that Amanda's husband possessed so that one day he followed his instincts and left home. Thus, Amanda views instinct as something bestial and vulgar. She wants a comfortable life within the bounds of prescribed propriety. Furthermore, Amanda refuses to recognize that her children have views different from hers.

F.

Amanda here is realist enough to know that Tom is reaching a point of desperation. She tells him that he can leave anytime after Laura is taken care of. Thus she returns to the theme of the gentleman caller and wants Tom to bring one home with the hopes that Laura can find some place of her own.

## SCENE FIVE

*Summary*

The scene opens with Amanda instructing Tom to comb his hair and not to smoke so much. Tom turns to the audience and tells about the Paradise Dance Hall across the alley and how adventure was to be found in other parts of the world. When Amanda sees the new moon, she makes a wish; this reminds Tom of Amanda's constant wish for a gentleman caller for Laura. He tells her that the gentleman caller is coming tomorrow. Amanda protests that she doesn't have time to get ready, but Tom tells her she shouldn't make a fuss over this boy. After Amanda finds out that his name is O'Connor, she decides to have a salmon loaf. She then inquires if Mr. O'Connor drinks because "old maids are better off than wives of drunkards!" Amanda asks how much money Mr. O'Connor makes a month and decides that eighty-five is just enough for a family man. She is very pleased to find out that he goes to night school and is trying to improve himself.

Tom finally warns Amanda that Mr. O'Connor doesn't yet know about Laura. Amanda thinks he will be glad he was invited to dinner when he sees how pretty and lovely Laura is. Tom tries to make Amanda see that Laura is different from other people. He doesn't want Amanda to expect too much from Laura. When he refers to her as crippled, Amanda reminds him that he is never to use that word. But Tom also means that Laura is different in other ways because "she lives in a world of her own—a world of—little glass ornaments" and old phonograph records. He then leaves to go to the movies. Amanda immediately calls Laura to come wish upon the moon and tells her to wish for "happiness" and "good fortune!"

*Commentary*

A.

As soon as Tom makes the momentous announcement that a gentleman caller is coming, Amanda begins immediately to make plans. As much as she has harped on the subject to Tom, she then begins to put him through a third degree and begins to find fault with Tom because he doesn't know enough about Jim O'Connor.

B.

Since Tom will be blamed for the evening's failure, we should note that Tom tells her there is no need to make a fuss for Mr. O'Connor. He also emphasizes that he doesn't know about Mr. O'Connor's private life. Thus Amanda's later accusations are falsely made.

C.

Note also Tom's futile attempt to make Amanda look at Laura realistically. She willfully ignores all of Tom's efforts to evaluate Laura realistically. She refuses to allow Tom to refer to Laura as crippled. But as Tom points out, Laura is more than crippled; she is a girl who lives in a world of little glass ornaments and old phonograph records. But Amanda refuses to recognize these and thinks only that this will be the gentleman caller who will marry Laura.

## SCENE SIX

*Summary*

Tom explains about Jim O'Connor. In high school, he had been the outstanding boy who had won basketball games and the silver cup in debating. But apparently his speed slowed down after graduation because he was holding a job not much better than Tom's. But Tom explains that Jim was his only friend at the warehouse because Tom was valuable to Jim's ego as a person who could remember his greatness in high school.

The scene then opens on Amanda and Laura as they are preparing for the arrival of the gentleman caller. Laura complains that her mother is making her nervous, but Amanda continues to fuss over Laura and even uses two powder puffs to pad Laura's breasts. Amanda goes away to dress herself and appears a little later wearing a very girlish frock held over from her youth and carrying a bunch of jonquils–"the legend of her youth." Amanda tells Laura that she is to open the door when Mr. O'Connor comes. Laura is taken aback by this name and when she hears that the first name is Jim, she tells Amanda that she won't be able to come to the dinner table. Since this would destroy all of Amanda's plans, she will not abide Laura's "silliness." Amanda disappears into the kitchen, and, when the doorbell rings, she calls merrily to Laura to answer the door. Laura begs her mother to open the door and tells her that she is sick. Amanda forces Laura to open the door. After she has let them in, Laura retreats as quickly as possible into the other room. Tom and Jim talk about the warehouse. Jim warns Tom that he is on the verge of losing his job, but Tom replies that his future plans don't include working at the warehouse. He has used the money for the last light bill to pay his dues at the Merchant Seaman's Union. But he warns Jim not to mention it because his mother doesn't yet know of his plans.

Amanda comes in and meets Jim O'Connor. She immediately bombards him with a long talk about weather, her gentlemen callers, and her past life. When Tom comes back from checking on the supper, he says that supper is already on the table and that Laura is not feeling well but Amanda refuses to begin supper until Laura comes. Laura enters and stumbles over a chair. Finally, Amanda notices that Laura is actually sick and tells Tom to help her to the living room. Laura lies shuddering on the couch while the others begin the evening meal.

*Commentary*

A.

Tom, in summing up Jim O'Connor, seems to see him as just a plain individual. Certainly during the course of the play, he shows no exceptional qualities. Quite the contrary, in the next scene, he will be seen as a rather blundering and awkward person.

B.

Notice that a large part of Laura's nervousness and sickness in this scene is brought about by Amanda's constant fretting and bothering. Laura even says to her: "Mother, you've made me so nervous." Again this shows Amanda's inability to understand her children. This is emphasized again when Amanda tells Laura that "you couldn't be satisfied with just sitting home." In reality, Laura would be quite content to remain home alone—she seems at this point to have no desire to meet other people.

C.

Before Jim O'Connor arrives, Amanda is busy changing into the dress that she wore when she met her husband. Again, it is difficult to know whether Amanda wants gentlemen callers for herself or for Laura. Certainly, she wants Laura to get married, but it will be seen to be Amanda who enjoys the idea of having the gentleman caller. She reverts back to her girlish days in both behavior and dress, and she appears with jonquils, the same flowers she carried the summer she met her husband.

D.

During the course of the conversation, Amanda mentions Mr. O'Connor's name. At this point Laura finds out that it is possibly the same Jim O'Connor she had a crush on in high school, and she tells Amanda that she will have to be excused. But Amanda will have no part of this "silliness." She forces Laura to open the door even though Laura is visibly agitated. Again, Amanda tries to make her children conform to her idea of behavior rather than letting them assert their own personalities.

E.

Notice here the stage direction. As soon as Laura opens the door, she rushes across the room to the phonograph. Her crossing the stage with her limp emphasizes her agitated state. Likewise, her retreat to the phonograph suggests her reliance upon her own world rather than meeting with the new world represented by the gentleman caller.

F.

Jim O'Connor's conversation about his course in public speaking again reveals him to be a rather prosaic character. By this point, it is rapidly becoming apparent that he is no great hero, except to Laura who remembers his great achievements during their high school days.

G.

This scene is the first definite evidence (outside of the prologue) that Tom is actually taking a step toward escaping from his present situation. He has used the money for the light bill in order to pay his dues with the Merchant Seaman's Union.

H.

Notice how Amanda, upon first meeting Jim O'Connor, almost overwhelms him with conversation. Here she displays all the "charm" that she can recapture.

I.

Again, ignoring Laura's feelings, Amanda forces Laura to come to the table. It is not until Laura stumbles and almost faints that Amanda finally realizes that Laura is actually sick.

## SCENE SEVEN

*Summary*

As the curtain rises, we see Laura still lying huddled on the sofa. Just as the others are finishing dinner, the lights go out, but Amanda calmly lights the candles and asks Jim if he would check on the fuses. She realizes that Tom probably didn't pay the light bill, so as punishment she makes him help with the dishes while Mr. O'Connor keeps Laura company. She asks him to take Laura a little wine to drink.

As Jim O'Connor approaches Laura, she sits up nervously. But Jim casually sits on the floor and asks Laura if she doesn't like to sit on the floor. He then chews some gum and offers her some. He asks her frankly why she is shy and refers to her as "an old-fashioned type of girl." When Laura asks him if he has kept up with his singing, Jim then remembers that they knew each other in high school. When Laura mentions that she was always late for their singing class because she was crippled and her brace clumped so loudly, Jim maintains that he never noticed it. He thinks that Laura was too self-conscious.

Laura brings out the high school year book which has pictures of Jim singing the lead role in an operetta. Laura tells Jim that she always wanted to ask him to autograph her book, but he was so terribly popular. Jim gallantly signs it for her now. When Laura asks Jim about his high school girl friend, he tells her that it was just rumor. Jim wonders what Laura has done since high school. She tells him about the business college and begins to tell about her glass collection; then Jim interrupts her and explains how she has an inferiority complex. When he finishes, Laura shows him her glass collection. Even though Jim is afraid that he will break one, Laura tells him that he can handle them. She even shows him her prize—her glass unicorn which is thirteen years old. Jim wonders if the unicorn doesn't feel strange since it is so different. Laura tells him that the unicorn doesn't complain and seems to get along nicely with the other animals.

Jim hears some music from the neighboring dance hall and asks Laura to dance. Even though she protests that she can't, Jim insists and during the dance, they stumble against the table and they break the horn off the unicorn. Laura maintains now that it is like the other horses. Jim tries to tell Laura how different she is—that she has a charm that is as different as "blue roses." He then says that someone should kiss Laura, and he leans over and kisses her. Almost immediately he knows that he has done the wrong thing, and he tells her that he shouldn't have kissed her because he is engaged to be married in the next month. After he finishes with his explanation, Laura gives him the broken unicorn. At this point Amanda enters with a pitcher of lemonade. After flitting about and chattering, she is about to leave when Jim explains that he has to go because he is engaged. Amanda is surprised and says that Tom didn't tell them that Jim was engaged. Jim explains that no one knows it yet, and then he leaves.

Amanda then calls Tom and accuses him of playing a joke on them by bringing home an engaged man. Even though Tom protests that he didn't know Jim was engaged, Amanda refuses to believe him. She holds Tom responsible for all of the expense involved in entertaining the gentleman caller and tells Tom that he is a selfish dreamer who never thinks about his "mother deserted and an unmarried sister who's crippled and has no job." So Tom does leave. But as the scene closes, Tom says that even though he left, he could never forget his sister. Wherever he goes, he still thinks about her.

*Commentary*

A.

During the first part of this scene, Amanda's conduct does show that she knows how to entertain and that she is not overly distracted by the lights going out. She is also very careful to use this as an excuse to get Tom into the kitchen so as to leave the gentleman caller with Laura.

B.

The scene between Laura and Jim O'Connor gives us our first view of Laura as a person. Suddenly, she comes alive as an individual, unique and different, but with her own charm that goes much deeper than the superficial gibbering of Amanda.

C.

Note that as the scene progresses, Laura rapidly gains confidence in herself and begins to lose some of her shyness. She relaxes enough to show Jim her glass menagerie, a collection that she treasures and that she would not readily show to just anyone. It is then that she explains her preference for the unicorn, which like Laura, is different from the other animals; its uniqueness makes it Laura's favorite. Symbolically, the unicorn here represents Laura's own self. She is also different and unique. But she, like the unicorn, doesn't complain about being lonesome or unique, and like Laura, the unicorn is the most delicate of all the animals in the collection.

D.

After looking at the collection, Jim proposes to Laura that they dance. He is still trying to build up her ego and to prove to her that she is not as different as she thinks herself to be. In other words, he is trying to break through to Laura. But the dance is used also as the method by which the unicorn is broken, and Jim's clumsiness can also break the delicate Laura.

E.

As soon as the unicorn is broken, Laura maintains that now it does not feel as freakish and looks more like the other horses. Symbolically, Laura is feeling more normal now than she has ever felt. Even though Jim seems to the audience a rather ordinary young man, to Laura he is quite exceptional, and he has achieved his aim of bringing Laura somewhat out of her world of retreat.

F.

After Jim makes his awkward confession about his engagement to Betty, Laura gives him the broken unicorn. Here the symbolism may be variously interpreted. We may see the broken unicorn as Laura's broken hopes, or we may say the broken unicorn is no longer unique like Laura but instead it is ordinary like Jim; or it may represent her broken hopes for love and romance, and she gives the symbol of her love to Jim to take away with him since he has broken her as well as her unicorn. That is, symbolically he takes away her broken unicorn and her broken love.

G.

Some people may wish to quarrel with the presentation of this scene in a memory play; that is, if the play is presented as Tom's memory, then he couldn't possibly know what took place in this scene.

H.

With Amanda's sudden attack on Tom for his allowing them to make such "fools of ourselves," we must remember that it was Tom who tried to get Amanda not to make a fuss, and that even Jim says Tom didn't know that he was engaged. But Amanda, realizing her own mistake, cannot take the blame for it. Suddenly, her charm leaves her, and we see her as just a nagging woman who cannot face reality. Here also her illusions leave her, and she even refers to Laura as "crippled."

# CHARACTER ANALYSES

## AMANDA WINGFIELD

Amanda Wingfield lives in a world that fluctuates between illusion and reality. When it is convenient to her, she simply closes her eyes to the brutal realistic world. She uses various escape mechanisms in order to endure her present position in life. When life in this tenement world becomes unbearable, she recalls the days of her youth when she lived at Blue Mountain and had seventeen gentlemen callers in one Sunday afternoon. Indeed, this story has been told so often that it is no longer an illusion and instead has become a reality. She likewise indulges in playful games so as to escape the drudgery of everyday living. She tells Laura, "You be the lady this time and I'll be the darky." She refuses to acknowledge that Laura is crippled and instead refers to her as having only a slight physical defect. She refuses to accept the fact that Tom is quite different from her and that he, like his father, will someday leave in search of adventures. And finally, Amanda lives perpetually in the world of the gentlemen callers who will appear any day to sweep Laura off her feet.

But she is unable to live forever in this world of illusion. The pressures of everyday living force her to face many unpleasant facts. Chief among these is the position of Laura. As she tells Laura: "I know so well what becomes of unmarried women who aren't prepared to occupy a position." Even if she fails to acknowledge Laura's defects, she is realist enough to understand Laura's difficult position. Furthermore, she has seen the letter that Tom received from the Merchant Marine and knows that he will soon be leaving. Facing these brutal facts, she makes Tom arrange to have the gentleman caller arrive.

But Amanda is full of other paradoxes. She wants only the best for her children, but then she fails to understand that what they most want is quite different from what she wants for them. She does gear her whole life toward their happiness because she doesn't want them to make the same mistakes that she made and yet in devoting herself to them, she has made herself overbearing and nagging.

Amanda's refusal to see that her children are quite different from her causes her many uncomfortable moments. She cannot understand why Laura cannot develop charm and gaiety but Amanda's idea of charm differs vastly from that of Laura's idea. Amanda can, at any moment, turn on a volley of chatter, be exceptionally lively and gay; Laura, on the other hand, lives in a quiet, sensitive world.

But Amanda possesses strong attributes. She does devote herself to her children. She does possess a great determination and strength. Many women could not have survived under the same situation. When she thinks a gentleman caller is coming, she sets herself to the task of preparation with a determination that cannot be equaled in her children.

If, in the final analysis, she is seen as giddy and frivolous, it is because life has passed her by. When her husband deserted her, she found herself faced with an empty and meaningless life. She then began to fabricate things with which to fill her life. She devoted herself too much to her children and began to live through her children. Since she was reliving her own life, she failed to understand the different personalities that her children possessed and ended up driving Tom away from home.

Thus Amanda is a person who lives alternately between a world of illusion and a world of reality. This fluctuation between these two worlds is her only defense against the boredom and emptiness of living.

## TOM WINGFIELD

Tom Wingfield was the potentially creative character caught in a conventional and materialistic world. He was the free spirit who had to curb his wings by working at a dreaded and disliked job in a shoe warehouse. Tom had his own independent world composed of those things he considered important—his poetry, his dreams, his freedom, his adventure, and his illusions. All these things were in direct opposition to his mother's world, but Tom's conflict was between his world and the realistic world. He was realist enough to recognize his sister's plight. He knew that his mother's dreams of gentlemen callers were false. He recognized that he had no future with the warehouse and he knew that he had to act without pity or else be destroyed as a sensitive being. He was forced, then, to leave his mother and sister or to be destroyed and consumed by their worlds of illusion, deception, and withdrawal.

For years, Tom had sought escape from Amanda's nagging inquisition and commands by attending movies almost nightly. This was his search for adventure. But Tom was soon to realize that he was watching adventure rather than living it. He realized, also, that the movies and drinking were only momentary psychological escapes. He used movies as a type of adventure to compensate for his own dull life and to escape from the nagging reminders of his everyday life. He needed escape from Amanda's domineering instructions as how to eat, when to eat, what to eat, how to quit smoking, how to improve himself, what to read, etc. When she began confiscating the books which he had brought home, his life became almost intolerable. If Amanda could not appreciate the greatness of an established creative genius, his own creative endeavors would never be understood or appreciated. Finally, when Tom tries to make his mother see that he is different from her, that he is not an exact reproduction of her own ideas, Amanda rejects the things which Tom stands for. Tom contended that "man is by instinct" a lover, a hunter, and a fighter. These are qualities which Amanda's husband possessed and she refused to recognize these qualities as decent. Therefore, Tom could only recognize his own instinctual drives by leaving home.

Tom, therefore, acted with painful honesty by committing himself to a life that excluded the shoe warehouse, the inert audiences in movie houses, and a direct and enervating contact with his family. Tom, being aware of the "boiling" within himself, knew that he had to act quickly or else be stifled by his environment. He realized that his own creative abilities and his sensitivity were being destroyed by his surroundings. Furthermore, he knew that if he didn't act, he would suffer regret, unhappiness, and a complete deterioration of his natural creative abilities.

Tom's rejection of his family was not a selfish egocentric escape. Instead, Tom recognized that he must escape in order to save himself. It was a means of self-preservation. He knew that if he stayed, he would be destroyed as a man and as an artist. But as man and artist, and as a sensitive individual, he has never been able to forget his life and especially the delicate charm and loveliness of his sister.

## LAURA WINGFIELD

Laura is presented as an extremely shy and sensitive person. Her shyness is emphasized even more by being contrasted with Amanda's forceful and almost brutal nature. We are made aware almost immediately of Laura's overly sensitive nature. She is so nervous that she cannot even attend business school without becoming violently sick. She is frightened and nervous when Tom and Amanda quarrel. She possesses a glass menagerie which she cares for with great tenderness. And she has withdrawn from the world—a withdrawal from what is real into what is make-believe.

Laura has a slight physical defect—a limp—but she has magnified this limp until it has affected her entire personality. Laura's oversensitive nature makes her think that everyone notices her limp; it becomes for her a huge stumbling block to normal living. She cannot get over it and into the real world. Her inability to overcome this defect causes her to withdraw into her world of illusion. The limp then becomes symbolic of Laura's inner nature. As Tom says, it's not just Laura's being crippled that makes her different, but she is just different. So she lives in a world of old phonograph records and glass animals.

And then the gentleman caller arrives. For the first time we see Laura's inner charm. She is fresh and pretty, and she does have charm—not as Amanda wants it, but in her own individualistic way. She is even capable of forgetting her physical handicap. She responds to Jim because he responds to her difference. With Jim, she sees that her difference is an asset and not a handicap. But ironically, she leads Jim more into her world than she enters into his. Thus, when the evening is over, when the unicorn is broken and the hopes are shattered, Laura does not have to retreat back into her world because she has never left it sufficiently enough to necessitate the retreat. Quite the contrary, now that the unicorn is broken, is ordinary like Jim, she sends it forth with Jim, and she remains in her unique world with the other unique glass animals.

## JIM O'CONNOR

In the character descriptions preceding the play, Jim is described as a "nice, ordinary, young man." He is the emissary from the world of normality. Yet this ordinary and simple person, seemingly out of place with the other characters, plays an important role in the climax of the play.

The audience is forewarned of Jim's character even before he makes his first appearance. Tom tells Amanda that the long-awaited gentleman caller is soon to come. Tom refers to Jim as a plain person, someone over whom there is no need to make a fuss. He earns only slightly more than does Tom and can in no way be compared to the magnificent gentlemen callers that Amanda used to have.

Jim's plainness is seen in his every action. He is interested in sports and does not understand Tom's more illusory ambitions to escape from the warehouse. His conversation shows him to be quite ordinary and plain. Thus, while Jim is the long-awaited gentleman caller, he is not a prize except in Laura's mind.

The ordinary aspect of Jim's character seems to come to life in his conversation with Laura. But it is contact with the ordinary that Laura needs. Thus it is not surprising that the ordinary seems to Laura to be the essence of magnificence. And since Laura had known Jim in high school when he was the all-American boy, she could never bring herself to look on him now in any way other than exceptional. He is the one boy that she has had a crush on. He is her ideal.

In the candlelight conversation with Laura, he becomes so wrapped up in reliving his own past that he seems once again to think that he is the high school hero who swept the girls off their feet.

He becomes so engrossed in the past that he not only breaks Laura's favorite piece of glass, but he also breaks Laura's dreams and hopes. He was so engrossed playing the role of high school hero and amateur psychiatrist that he failed to see what emotions he was building up in Laura. His most accurate description of himself is when he refers to himself as a "stumble-john."

But Jim's function in the play is more important then his seemingly ordinary character would allow. Since Laura lives in a world of illusion and dream, Jim, as the ordinary person, seems to Laura to be wonderful and exceptional. He is so different from her own world that he appears to be the knight in shining armor.

## QUESTIONS

1. How does the fire escape function as a symbol to reveal something about each character's personality? (See commentary after the first scene.)

2. Why does Tom go so often to the movies? (See character analysis of Tom.)

3. What are the similarities between Tom and his father? (See commentary after Scene Four and the character analyses of Amanda and Tom.)

4. What is the significance of Laura's unicorn? (See commentary after Scene Seven.)

5. Why does Amanda nag at Tom so much? (See commentary after Scenes One, Three and Four.)

6. Why does Laura give the unicorn to Jim? (See commentary after Scene Seven.)

7. Why does it take Tom so long to decide to leave home? (See character analysis of Tom and commentary after Scene Five.)

8. Does Jim have the potential greatness attributed to him by Laura? (See commentary after Scene Seven.)

9. Does Laura fully understand her position and especially the responsibility that Tom feels for her? (See character analysis of Laura and commentary after Scenes Two and Three.)

10. Why does Amanda blame Tom for the failure of the evening? (See commentary after Scene Seven.)

## SUGGESTED THEME TOPICS

1. Choose either Laura, Tom, or Amanda, and argue how the person you chose should be considered the main character of the play.

2. Write a theme characterizing Williams' views toward illusion and reality.

3. Which characters face life most realistically? Defend your choice.

4. Write an essay depicting Amanda's strengths and weakness. Is she an admirable person or merely a silly frustrated woman?

# A STREETCAR NAMED DESIRE

*By Tennessee Williams*

## PLOT SUMMARY

Blanche DuBois arrives to visit her sister, Mrs. Stella Kowalski, who lives in the French Quarter of New Orleans. She is shocked by the disreputable looks of the place. While a neighbor goes to find Stella, Blanche looks around the apartment for a drink. When her sister comes, Blanche quite frankly criticizes the place. She explains that she has come for a visit because her nerves are shattered from teaching. Noticing that the apartment has only two rooms, she has qualms about staying but she tells Stella that she can't stand being alone.

She explains to Stella that their old ancestral home, Belle Reve, has been lost. While Stella goes to the bathroom, Stanley, her husband, enters and meets Blanche. He questions her about her past and especially about her earlier marriage, which upsets Blanche to the point that she feels sick.

The following night Stella and Blanche plan to have dinner out and go to a movie while Stanley plays poker with his friends. But before they leave, Stanley wants to know how Belle Reve was lost. Blanche tries to explain and gives him all the papers and documents pertaining to the place. Later that night when Blanche and Stella return from their movie, the men are still playing poker. Blanche meets Mitch, one of Stanley's friends, who seems to be more sensitive than the others. While Mitch is in the second room talking to Blanche, Stanley becomes angry over a series of incidents, especially when Blanche turns on the radio. He throws the radio out the window, hits Stella when she tries to stop him, and has to be held by the other men to be kept from doing more damage. Blanche takes Stella and runs upstairs. When Stanley recovers, he calls for Stella to come down and she does.

The next morning, Blanche goes to Stella and tries to make her see that Stanley is an animal. She is shocked that Stella could have returned to him. But Stella assures her that Stanley was gentle when she returned and that she loves him. As Blanche begins describing Stanley, he comes in and overhears the conversation but doesn't say a thing.

Some time later, Blanche is dressing for a date with Mitch. She tells Stella that she wants Mitch because she is so tired of struggling against the world. Stella assures her it will happen. She leaves with Stanley to go bowling; just before Mitch arrives a paper boy comes by and Blanche detains him long enough to kiss him because he reminds her of her young husband. When Blanche and Mitch return from their date, Blanche explains to Mitch how much Stanley apparently hates her. She thinks that Stanley will be her destroyer. She tells Mitch about her past life, how once she was married to a young boy whom she later discovered with an older man. Later that night, her young husband killed himself as a result of a harsh remark that Blanche made to him. Mitch tells Blanche that they both need each other.

It is later in mid-September. Stella is preparing a birthday cake for Blanche. Stanley comes home and tells Stella that he now has the lowdown on Blanche. It seems that she lived such a wild life in Laurel that she was asked to leave the town. Even the army had referred to Blanche as being out-of-bounds. Stanley then tells her that Mitch won't be coming over and that Blanche will leave Tuesday on the Greyhound bus. Later that evening Blanche cannot understand why Mitch does not come. After a scene between Stanley and Stella, Stanley gives Blanche her birthday present—the ticket back to Laurel, Mississippi. As Stanley is about to leave, Stella has her first labor pains and has to be taken to the hospital.

Mitch arrives later that evening. Blanche has been drinking rather heavily. He confronts her with her past life. At first she tries to deny it, but then she confesses that after the death of her young husband, nothing but intimacies with strangers seemed to have any meaning for her. Mitch then tries to get her to sleep with him, and Blanche demands marriage. Mitch tells her she is not good enough, and Blanche screams *fire* so as to make Mitch leave.

Later that night Stanley returns from the hospital to find Blanche dressed in an old faded evening dress. He tells her that the baby won't come before morning. She is frightened to stay with him, especially when he begins confronting her with all the lies she has told. As she tries to move around him, he decides that she wouldn't be too bad to interfere with. After a scuffle, he rapes her.

Three weeks later, Stella is packing Blanche's clothes and waiting for a doctor and an attendant to come and take her to the state mental institution. Stella refuses to believe Blanche's story that Stanley raped her. Blanche thinks that an old boy friend is coming to take her on a cruise. When the attendant arrives, she doesn't recognize him and tries to run away. Stanley and an assistant trap Blanche. The doctor approaches and Blanche is quite willing to go with him, having always depended on the kindness of strangers.

## CENTRAL CHARACTERS

*Blanche DuBois*

A sensitive delicate moth-like member of the fading Southern aristocracy who has just lost her teaching position as a result of her promiscuity.

*Stella Kowalski*

Blanche's sister who is married and lives in the French Quarter of New Orleans. She has forgotten her genteel upbringing in order to enjoy a more common marriage.

*Stanley Kowalski*

A rather common working man whose main drive in life is sexual and who faces everything with brutal realism.

*Harold Mitchell (Mitch)*

Stanley's friend who went through the war with him. Mitch is unmarried and has a dying mother for whom he feels a great devotion.

*Eunice and Steve Hubell*

The neighbors who quarrel and who own the apartment in which Stella and Stanley live.

## STRUCTURE THROUGH CONTRASTS

The structure of this play is best seen through a series of confrontations between Blanche DuBois and Stanley Kowalski. In the first scene the confrontation is not so severe, but it increases in severity until one of the two must be destroyed. To understand fully the scenes of confrontations, the reader should have a good understanding of what is at stake in each encounter. That is, he should understand some of the differences between the DuBois world and the Kowalski world.

The most obvious difference between the worlds of Blanche DuBois and Stanley Kowalski lies in the diversity of their backgrounds. We immediately recognize that the very name DuBois and Kowalski contrast. Williams has begun to sketch the personalities by a nationality association. We assume DuBois to be an aristocratic name, possibly one with a proud heritage. A DuBois wouldn't be found working in a steel mill, as would a Kowalski. A DuBois speaks softly and flittingly. A Kowalski speaks loud and brutally. Kowalskis relish loud poker parties with their characteristic rough humor. Blanche DuBois winces at this. Her preferences for entertainment are teas, cocktails, and luncheons. Speech, to Stanley, is a way of expressing his wants, likes, and dislikes. Blanche speaks on a higher level. She searches for values, reflecting education in her manner of speaking. Kowalski regards money as the key to happiness; money will buy anything. Stanley's interest in Belle Reve centers only upon the fact that under the Napoleonic Code he loses money. He cares nothing for the tradition of the place but only its financial value. Money to his type is a power that can buy some basic wants or pleasures of life. This gives him a type of animal superiority to the world of people (like the DuBois) who do not understand the value of money and then become destitute.

Stanley and Blanche, as individual representatives of these two worlds, show even more contrasts in their personalities. The use of color differs remarkably. Stanley needs vividness to prove his physical manhood. He is presented "as coarse and direct and powerful as the primary colors." His green and scarlet bowling shirt is an example. Blanche shuns loud shades and selects pastels or white. The directness of bright colors repulses her; she prefers muted, muffled tones.

Another contrast arises in the comparison of their zodiac signs. Stanley was born in December under Capricorn the Goat. This brings to mind many obvious associations in connection with Stanley's personality. Blanche's sign is Virgo, the virgin. True, she is a very degenerate "virgin," but in body only. She tries to keep the mentality of a virgin. She believes she is a virgin because the men she has slept with have meant nothing to her; they have not actually taken from her. She has not given of her real self to them. But to represent herself in such a manner seems a direct lie to the Kowalski world. There can be no such subtle difference in the Kowalski world. This leads to one of the central conflicts of the play, Blanche's honesty versus her seeming dishonesty.

A Kowalski, as seen in Stanley, is "simple, straightforward, and honest." He tolerates nothing but the bare unembellished truth. Blanche, so to speak, "puts a gaily-colored paper lantern" on the harshness of truth. This isn't lying to her. A lie, for Blanche, would be a betrayal of herself, of everything she believes in. Therefore, it would not only be a verbal lie but also a lie in act. Stanley abhors the paper lantern. He accepts it for nothing other than a lie and detests Blanche for deceiving others with it. This conflict is irresolvable because it originates in the essence of their personalities. To concede to the other's view entails self-destruction.

Love is essential to both worlds but has entirely different significance for each. Stanley needs love to satisfy his animal desires. To him it is the physical act of love, no more. Blanche's sensitivity is the key to her approach to love. She needs someone not to fulfill her basic physical desires but to protect her or she feels the need of giving herself to someone. Her concept of love is on a higher level than Stanley's. Shunning the brutality and animality of a Kowalski, she seeks some type of communication, some capacity for devotion.

Desire isn't the lustful passion that Stanley regards it, but it is a spiritual need. Speaking of Mitch, Stella asks her, "Blanche, do you want him?" She answers, "I want to rest. I want to breathe quietly again." She seeks security and protection for her sensitiveness against the rough edges of her surroundings.

The symbol employed most frequently by Williams in his emphasis of the essential differences in the worlds is light. It represents the reality Stanley lives by and the harshness Blanche must soften. He faces it because it is him; he is "a naked light bulb." He faces the way things are, doesn't delude himself into believing they are something else. Blanche did that once when she saw the truth about her young husband, and it nearly broke her. Since then she has retired into a world of shadow and illusion. "There has never been any light that's stronger than this—kitchen—candle." If she must have a light, she prefers candlelight. The light in her room is too strong for her; so she covers it with a paper lantern. She uses this in a symbolic explanation of her own approach to reality: "soft people have got to court the favour of hard ones...have got to be seductive—put on soft colors...shimmer and glow." This then is the only way in which Blanche can cope with Stanley's world, but his world forbids it. She must improvise, make the necessary adjustments. He tolerates no compromise. His primitive, honest manner threatens to destroy her. The two ways of life are totally incompatible; there can be no peaceful coexistence.

Thus the play is structured on the principle of presenting the two worlds, establishing what each world believes in, and then placing these worlds in a series of direct confrontations until one is destroyed.

## SCENE SUMMARIES AND COMMENTARIES

### SCENE ONE

*Summary*

Stanley appears and calls for Stella, his wife, to catch a package of meat. He then goes bowling and Stella follows. Almost immediately, Blanche appears trying to find a certain street number. Eunice, the neighbor, sees that Blanche is confused and assures her that this is the place where Stella lives. Eunice lets Blanche into the apartment and goes after Stella. Immediately, Blanche finds a bottle of whiskey and gulps down a big swig.

When Stella arrives, Blanche blurts out how awful the apartment is but then tries to laugh off her comment. She asks for a drink in order to restore her nerves. Blanche then returns to the subject of the apartment, wondering how Stella could live in such a place. Stella tries to explain that New Orleans is different and that the apartment is not so bad. Blanche promises to say no more about it.

Blanche explains to Stella that she had to resign from her high school teaching position because of her nerves. It was so sudden that she wasn't able to let Stella know about it. Blanche notices that the apartment only has two rooms and she wonders where she will sleep. Stella shows her the folding bed and explains that Stanley won't mind the lack of privacy because he is Polish. And Stella warns Blanche that Stanley's friends are not the type Blanche is accustomed to.

Blanche emphasizes that she must stay for a while because she can't stand to be alone. This leads Blanche to tell Stella that Belle Reve, the ancestral home, has been lost. When Stella asks how it happened, Blanche reminds Stella how there has been a long line of deaths in the family and that she had to stay there and fight while Stella was "in bed with your—Polack." When Stella begins crying and goes to the bathroom, Blanche hears Stanley outside. Blanche introduces herself to him. Stanley takes off his shirt so as to be comfortable and offers Blanche a drink but Blanche says that she rarely touches it. Stanley asks Blanche if she wasn't once married. Blanche tells him yes, but the boy died; then, she leaves thinking that she is going to be sick.

*Commentary*

A.

The first part of this scene introduces us symbolically to the essential characteristics of Stanley Kowalski. He enters in a loud colored bowling jacket and work clothes, and is carrying "a red-stained package." He bellows to Stella and throws her the raw meat which she catches as she laughs breathlessly. The neighbors laugh over the package of bloody meat – an obvious sexual symbol which depicts Stanley in the same way as Blanche later describes him to Stella: He is a "survivor of the strong age! Bearing the raw meat home from the kill in the jungle; and you – you here – waiting for him." This scene, therefore, shows Stanley as the crude and uncouth man. The scene also sets a tone of commonplace brutality and reality into which the delicate and sensitive Blanche is about to appear.

B.

Williams is overly fond of using Freudian sexual symbols. The reader should be aware of these and choose his own response. Aside from the use of the raw meat, he uses the bowling balls and pins, and the columns of the Belle Reve plantation home as obvious overt phallic and sexual symbols. The fact that Stanley bowls suggests symbolically his characteristic of summing everything up in terms of sexuality.

C.

When Blanche says that she took a "streetcar named Desire, and then...one called Cemeteries," Williams seems to be implying that desire leads to death which is then an escape to the Elysian Fields. But ironically, in terms of the play, the streetcar leads her to the French Quarter which is certainly no Elysian Fields.

D.

Notice that Blanche is described as wearing white and having a moth-like appearance. Williams often dresses his most degenerate characters in white, the symbol of purity. (For example, aside from Blanche, Chance Wayne in *Sweet Bird of Youth* and Sebastian in *Suddenly, Last Summer* are always dressed in white.) Blanche's dress hides her inner sins and contributes to her moth-like appearance. Her actions also suggest the fluttering of a delicate moth. And as a moth is often attracted by light and consequently killed by the heat, later we will see that Blanche is afraid of the light and when Mitch forces her under the light, this act begins Blanche's destruction.

E.

Note the symbolic use of names throughout the play. Blanche DuBois means white of the woods. The white is a play on Blanche's supposed innocence and the woods are used as another Freudian phallic symbol. Stella's name means star. The name of the plantation home was Belle Reve or beautiful dream – thus the loss of Belle Reve is correlated with the loss of a beautiful dream that Blanche once possessed.

F.

In the first meeting between Stella and Blanche, Blanche tells Stella to "turn that over-light off!" This is a first reference to Blanche's aversion to too much light. It correlates with her moth-like appearance and will later develop into one of the controlling motifs throughout the play. Her fear of light will be seen to be connected with the death of her first husband and her fear of being too closely examined in the cold hard world of reality. She prefers, instead, the dim, illusionary world of semi-darkness.

G.

A key to Blanche's character is given to us in this first scene by her reliance upon and need for whiskey. Then later when Stanley asks her if she wants a drink, she tells him that she rarely touches it. Here then is an example of Blanche's inability to tell the truth and her desire to be something different from what she actually is.

H.

Blanche's emphasis that she can't be alone suggests that she is at a point of desperation at the opening of the play. She has absolutely no place to go and no one to turn to or else she would not be here in these surroundings. Her explanation of how Belle Reve was lost and her recountings of her frequent encounters with death serve in some ways to account for Blanche's present neurotic state.

I.

The reader should be especially aware of Williams' description of Stanley. "Animal joy in his being is implicit in all his movements." This is the opposite of the delicate and ethereal Blanche. Furthermore, the "center of his life has been pleasure with women." He is the "emblem of the gaudy seed-bearer." He takes pride in everything that is *HIS*. Thus part of the later conflict is that Blanche can never in any sense of the word be *HIS*. She lives in his house, eats his food, drinks his liquor, criticizes his life, etc., but she is never his. Blanche's refusal will later help us understand the reasons for the brutal rape.

J.

Essentially, the play can be read as a series of encounters between the Kowalski world and the Blanche DuBois world. Each of these encounters will intensify with each subsequent meeting. The first encounter occurs at the end of Scene One. The overly sensitive Blanche must introduce herself to Stanley, who immediately offers her a drink after he notices that the bottle has been touched. He takes off his shirt and makes a shady remark to Stella, who is in the bathroom. He then asks Blanche some pointed questions which end with an inquiry about her earlier marriage. By the end of the first encounter, Blanche is feeling sick. Thus, Stanley's rough, common, brutal questions end by hitting on the most sensitive aspect of Blanche's past life—her marriage with the young boy. Stanley's animalism almost destroys Blanche's sensibilities even in this first meeting. Thus the conflict is between the oversensitive aristocratic world of Blanche and the brutal, realistic, present-day world represented by Stanley. But as an afternote, it should be added that Stanley is the type of person who likes his "cards on the table." He doesn't go in for subtleties and deception; thus, had Blanche been honest about his liquor, perhaps they could have gotten off to a better start.

## SCENE TWO

### *Summary*

Stella tells Stanley that she is taking Blanche out for dinner and a show while he has his poker game at the apartment. He is annoyed because he has to eat a cold plate which Stella placed in the ice box. She tells him that they have lost Belle Reve and that Blanche is upset and it would help if Stanley could admire Blanche's dress. But Stanley wants to return to the loss of Belle Reve. He wants to see a bill of sale or some papers. He reminds Stella of the Napoleonic Code which states that anything belonging to the wife belongs also to the husband. Thus if the wife is swindled, then the husband is swindled and Stanley does not like to be swindled. Stanley looks at all the furs and jewelry Blanche has brought with her and demands to know where the money came from to buy these. Stella tries to explain that it is all just artificial stuff and very cheap. But Stanley is going to have a friend evaluate it all. Stella goes out on the porch so as to end the discussion.

When Blanche comes from her hot bath, she asks Stanley to button her and to give her a drag on his cigarette. He begins to question her about the clothes and Blanche begins fishing for a compliment from him about her looks. He tells her that he doesn't go in for that sort of thing and only likes people who "lay their cards on the table." Stella tries to stop the discussion, but Blanche sends her out after a coke. Then Stanley asks her about the loss of Belle Reve. Blanche explains that she knows she fibs a lot, because "after all, a woman's charm is fifty percent illusion," but when something is important she always tells the truth. Stanley asks her for the papers. She goes to the trunk and hands him a tin box. He wants to know what the other papers are and at the same time snatches them. Blanche tells him that they are love letters and the touch of his hands insults them. She then gives him the papers from many firms which had made loans on the plantation and comments that it is fitting all these old papers should now be in his hands. He takes the papers and tries to justify his suspicion by saying he has to be careful now that Stella is going to have a baby. When Stella returns, Blanche tells her how happy she is about the baby and how well she handled Stanley and that she even flirted with him. They leave as the poker players begin to arrive.

*Commentary*

A.

The first part of this scene introduces us to the motif of Blanche's baths. She bathes constantly so as to soothe her nerves. But this is also a cleansing symbol. By her baths, she sub-consciously hopes to cleanse her sins away. The baths are also another quirk which annoys Stanley since the hot baths make the apartment even hotter.

B.

Note the open and flagrant manner in which Blanche flirts with Stanley. Again the buttons, the request for a drag on his cigarette, and the trunk function as favorite Freudian symbols. Here they are used to reinforce the idea that Blanche is attempting symbolically to seduce Stanley. She is so open about it that Stanley says "If I didn't know that you was my wife's sister I'd get ideas about you." This scene therefore balances with the later scene when Stanley rapes Blanche.

C.

Blanche's attempt to flirt with Stanley is her only known way of achieving success with men. She tries to use her charms. Actually, she wants Stanley to admire her and willingly commits a breach of decorum when she attempts this symbolic seduction.

D.

This second scene presents the second encounter between the Stanley and Blanche worlds. Here even Blanche recognizes that Stanley's world is destructive to people like her. She says of her husband: "I hurt him the way that you would like to hurt me, but you can't." But in actuality, Stanley will be able to destroy her rather easily. Blanche also recognizes the difference between the two worlds when she presents Stanley the collected papers of Belle Reve and thinks that it is fitting their papers for the aristocratic home should now be in his brutal hands. At the end of the encounter, it is Blanche who is left trembling and shaken by the encounter.

## SCENE THREE

*Summary*

Later that night Mitch, Stanley's friend, wants to drop out of the poker game because his mother is sick. Stella and Blanche return from the show, and Blanche is introduced to the other players. When Stanley tells the ladies to disappear until the game is finished,

Stella reminds him that it is 2:30 A.M. and time to quit. Stanley swats her rear and the sisters go into the other room where Blanche meets Harold Mitchell coming from the bathroom. When he leaves, Blanche thinks that he looks more sensitive than the others and is told that Mitch's mother is very sick. Blanche begins to undress until Stella reminds her that she is in the light. The sisters begin to laugh, and Stanley yells to them to be quiet. When Stella goes to the bathroom, Blanche moves back into the light and continues to undress as she listens to rumba music over the radio. Stanley calls for her to turn the radio off. Mitch excuses himself again and goes into the other room where he meets Blanche again. She asks him for a cigarette, and he shows her his cigarette case with an inscription on it. Blanche recognizes the inscription and Mitch is pleased and explains that there is a story connected with the case. It was given to him by a girl who was dying and knew it when she gave him the present. Blanche explains that people who suffer are often more sensitive and sincere than the average person. Blanche asks Mitch to cover the light bulb with a paper lantern because she can't "stand a naked light bulb, any more than a rude remark or a vulgar action." After more conversation, Blanche explains how she tried to teach English and an appreciation for literature to youngsters who were not interested in it. As Stella comes out of the bathroom, Blanche turns on the radio and begins a little waltz, and Mitch clumsily tries to follow when suddenly Stanley charges into the room and throws the radio out the window. Stella screams at him and tells everyone to go home. Stanley becomes enraged and hits Stella. The men pin Stanley down while the women leave. They force him under the shower and then leave. Stanley emerges and calls Eunice and asks to speak to Stella. He threatens to keep on calling until he talks with Stella. Then he goes outside and bellows for her. Eunice comes out and tells him to be quiet because Stella is not coming down. He continues to yell for her, and Stella emerges from the apartment and comes slowly to him. He falls to his knees and presses her against him. He then carries her back into the apartment. Blanche comes looking for Stella. She sees Mitch who explains that Stella went back to him. Mitch assures her that all is fine now. Blanche looks at him and thanks him for being so kind.

*Commentary*

A.

Note that the scene is set against a pretty wild poker game. Stanley is especially out of patience because he has been losing heavily. And we see Mitch immediately as a contrast to the others, especially with his concern for his sick mother.

B.

Blanche is immediately aware of Mitch's difference. Her own sensitivity allows her to recognize it in others. This is a quality that Stanley does not possess.

C.

Blanche intentionally moves into the light when she is undressing so as to be noticed. This is a manifestation of Blanche's desire to be the center of attention, and her use of her body to attract attention prepares us for some of her later lurid escapades.

D.

Notice that Blanche's and Mitch's pasts curiously correspond since both have lost a loved person. This is just one of many aspects that will draw them together.

E.

Again the light motif is here developed. Blanche asks Mitch to cover the naked light bulb. Ironically, it will be he who will later tear off the paper lantern in order to "get a better look" at Blanche.

F.

The reader should be aware of Blanche's almost pathological need to lie. She lies to Mitch about her reason for visiting Stella and about her age. But as Blanche will later say, these are only little illusions that a woman must create.

G.

This is the third confrontation between Blanche and Stanley. Here Blanche is the witness to the animal brutality and the coarse behavior of Stanley. The violence that he perpetrates is totally alien to Blanche's understanding. But more amazing to Blanche is the fact that Stella returns to Stanley after the fight is over.

H.

In Stella's return to Stanley when he calls for her, we see the basis on which their marriage is built. In earlier scenes it was intimated that there could be no similiar traits between them. Here it becomes apparent that the basic attraction is one of pure physical sexual attractions as they "come together with low, animal moans."

I.

What is often overlooked in this scene is the basic cause of this scene. To project, one must ask himself, would this outburst have occurred if Blanche had not been visiting there. It is apparent that Blanche's presence was the principal cause of the violence. And later it will be developed that Stanley feels her presence is an actual threat to his marriage.

J.

The attraction between Mitch and Blanche contrasts aptly to the bestial attraction between Stanley and Stella. The sensitivity and the quietness of Blanche and Mitch emphasize the delicate basis of their relationship.

## SCENE FOUR

*Summary*

The following morning, Blanche comes hesitantly and frightenedly to the Kowalski apartment and when she sees Stella alone, she rushes to her and embraces her. Stella tells Blanche to stop being so excitable. Blanche cannot understand how Stella could have returned to Stanley last night. Stella assures her that he was tame as a lamb. She tries to convince Blanche that she is quite content and happy in her present situation. Blanche ignores her and tries to think of some way of getting them out of the situation even though Stella repeatedly says she doesn't want out. Blanche remembers an old boy friend named Shep Huntleigh. She plans to contact him to see if he can help her out of her situation. She tells Stella that she has only 65¢ to her name, but she feels that after what happened last night she can't live under the same roof with Stanley. Stella tries to explain that Stanley was at his worst last night.

Through all of Blanche's attacks, Stella remains calm, and simply asserts that she loves Stanley. Then Blanche asks if she may speak plainly. At this moment, Stanley enters the room unheard by Blanche and Stella, and he overhears Blanche's comments. Blanche says that Stanley is common and bestial. He has animal habits and is a "survivor of the Stone Age." She pleads with Stella to remember some of the advances of civilization and not to "hang back with the brutes." At this point, Stanley leaves quietly and calls from outside. When he comes in, Stella throws herself into his arms.

*Commentary*

A.

This scene points up Blanche as the definite outsider. In attempting to get Stella to see Stanley as a common and bestial person, she succeeds only in alienating herself from Stella.

B.

Blanche begins to feel her desperate situation. Here she first conceives of contacting her old acquaintance, Shep Huntleigh, who will develop as a symbol of her potential escape from this world.

C.

Blanche's view of Stanley, that he is common and bestial—a survivor of the Stone Age bearing home the raw meat from the kill—does characterize the essential nature of Stanley. It should be remembered that the first scene showed Stanley bringing home a package of raw meat and tossing it to Stella. And Blanche's description also serves to illustrate how utterly different he is from the type of man Blanche has known.

D.

This scene does not give us a direct confrontation between Blanche and Stanley, but instead and equally important, there is a confrontation between the two concepts of life represented by

Stanley and Blanche. And at the end of the scene when Stella throws herself at Stanley, it is an obvious victory for Stanley.

E.

Even though Stanley feels victorious in this encounter, we must remember that he has overheard himself referred to as common, bestial, and vulgar. Blanche has called him a *savage* and a brute. This has occurred in *his* own home. Therefore, his resentment of Blanche and desire to be rid of her is quite justifiable. Later when he rapes her, the rape will be partially motivated by his resentment of her attitude toward him.

## SCENE FIVE

### *Summary*

Blanche has been visiting now for three months. She has just finished composing a letter to Shep Huntleigh pretending that she has been on a round of teas and cocktail parties. Stanley comes in and is apparently irritated. He is antagonistic toward Blanche. When he goes about slamming drawers, she asks him what astrological sign he was born under. We find out that Stanley was born under the sign of Capricorn (the Goat) and Blanche was born under Virgo (the Virgin). Stanley laughs contemptuously when he hears this and then abruptly asks her about a man named Shaw who had known Blanche in a Hotel Flamingo. Blanche asserts that the Flamingo is not the sort of place where she would be seen. Stanley says that he will have this man check it out and "clear up any mistake." At this point Blanche is about ready to faint. Stanley leaves to go bowling after refusing to kiss Stella in front of Blanche.

Immediately, Blanche wonders if Stella has heard some unkind gossip about her. Blanche explains that in the last few years after she began to lose Belle Reve she was too soft and was not strong enough, and there were some stories spread around about her. Stella brings her a coke and tells her to quit talking morbidly. Blanche promises to leave before Stanley pitches her out, but by now she is shaking so badly that the coke foams and spills on her dress. She screams piercingly and Stella wonders why. Blanche explains that she is nervous because Mitch is coming for her at seven. She tells Stella that she has created an illusion with Mitch that she is all prim and proper. She has also lied about her age because she wants Mitch to want her. Stella asks if Blanche is interested in Mitch. She tells Stella that she wants to rest and that she does want Mitch. Stanley calls for Stella and as she is leaving, she assures Blanche that her wish for Mitch will come true, but that Blanche should not drink any more.

In a few minutes, a young man comes to the door. He is collecting for the paper. He is about to leave when Blanche tells him that she has no money, but she calls him back and asks for a light. Then she asks him about the rain and what he did when it rained. He told her that he went in the drug store and had a cherry soda. He tries to leave again but Blanche stops him, telling him how handsome he looks and then she walks over and kisses him softly on the lips. She then sends him away saying that she must keep her hands off children. A few minutes later Mitch appears with a bunch of roses.

*Commentary*

A.

Note that as soon as Blanche says that she was born under the sign of the virgin, Stanley chooses this moment to ask her about the man named Shaw. Blanche becomes visibly agitated during the cross-examination. At the end, when Stanley leaves, she is trembling and in need of a drink. This, then, is Blanche's past life beginning to close in upon her. This is also the beginning of Stanley's plan to destroy Blanche, and she feels herself being trapped. Thus in this encounter between Blanche and Stanley, Blanche is seeing her own valued world disintegrate under the force of Stanley's attack.

B.

This scene also illustrates Williams' fondness for the use of symbols. The astrological signs, the spilled coke on Blanche's white dress, and the cherry soda that the young man mentions are all used as slightly suggestive symbols.

C.

At this point in the drama, the scene with the young boy might seem puzzlingly out of place. It is not until later that we learn Blanche had once married a young boy and had been terribly cruel to him when he most needed her. Therefore, her sexual promiscuity returns to her guilt feelings over her failure to help her young husband. She seeks to relive the past and longs for a young lover to replace the young husband who shot himself. In other words, since she once denied help to her young husband, she now tries to compensate by giving herself to almost anyone.

## SCENE SIX

### *Summary*

Later that same evening, Blanche and Mitch are returning rather late from a date. They are discussing the failure of the evening. Blanche takes the blame for the failure because she feels that it is the lady's duty to "entertain the gentleman." After Blanche tells Mitch that she must soon pack her trunks, he asks her permission to kiss her goodnight. Blanche tells him he should not have to ask, but warns him that he is to go no further because a single girl has to be so careful.

Stanley and Stella are not at home and Blanche asks Mitch to come in for a nightcap. While Blanche is looking for some whiskey, she lights a candle and says in French that she is the lady of the camellias. When Mitch says he does not understand French, Blanche asks him in French if he would like to sleep with her and then says in English that it's a damned good thing that he doesn't understand French. She asks him to take off his coat, but he is ashamed of the way he sweats. He tells her how heavy he is and how easily he sweats, but Blanche maintains that he is just a good healthy man.

Mitch asks where Stella and Stanley are. He then suggests that the four of them should go out together sometime; Blanche explains how much Stanley hates her and wonders if he has told Mitch anything. Mitch pretends that he hasn't, but Blanche feels uneasy. She explains how rude and common he is to her and that as soon as Stella has the baby, she is going to leave. Blanche is convinced that Stanley hates her, and that "that man will destroy me."

Mitch suddenly asks Blanche how old she is. Blanche wonders why, and Mitch tells her that he has talked about her to his mother. Blanche wonders if Mitch won't be very lonely when he loses his mother. She explains that she knows what loneliness is because she once lost a person she loved. He was just a boy when they married, and he had a softness and tenderness which she did not fully understand. Then she found out that the boy she had married was also having an affair with an older man. She found out by coming into the room where they were. Pretending nothing had happened, the three of them went to a dance, where suddenly Blanche told her young husband that he disgusted her. He ran from her and immediately shot himself. Since that time, there has been no light in her life stronger than the kitchen candle.

Mitch responds that she needs somebody and that he does too. Thus as the polka tune which has been playing in Blanche's mind during her narration stops, she and Mitch embrace.

### *Commentary*

**A.**

This scene presents the hope, the sense of salvation for Blanche. It follows the tradition of classical tragedy in the way that a classical tragedy always allows for the possibility of redemption sometime in the middle of the play. Blanche's hope lies with her capturing Mitch, and it will later be Stanley's revelation about Blanche's past to Mitch which finally destroys all of Blanche's hopes. But here in this scene, it seems as though Blanche may succeed in freeing herself from her trapped situation.

**B.**

An important question is, which is the real Blanche? Is she the innocent naïve girl that she presents to Mitch or is she the depraved woman whose past Stanley uncovers and reveals? Actually, she would like to be the girl she is presenting to Mitch. Ideally, she pictures herself as this girl. Even though this is a pose for her, she feels that it is the pose that she, as the southern belle, must take. Like Amanda Wingfield in *The Glass Menagerie*, she feels it is her duty to entertain the man and to make the man feel welcomed.

C.

When Mitch discusses his excessive weight, his sweating, and his clumsiness, we must see Mitch as a rough sort of man. He is no diamond in the raw. In other words, he is Blanche's last chance. He is the last straw which she is grasping for so as to keep from drowning.

D.

This scene also shows that Blanche realizes Stanley is her "executioner." – "That man will destroy me, unless" – the "unless" refers to her hope of marrying Mitch. But here she recognizes that Stanley is deliberately trying to destroy her, and she can't do much about it.

E.

In Blanche's narration of her tragic marriage with the young Allan, we see the source of all the rest of her difficulties. Here was the man whom she loved "unendurable" but whom she was unable to help. Her love came like a "blinding light" and after his death, she has never had a light "that's stronger than this – kitchen – candle!" Thus, Blanche's aversion to lights, seen in earlier parts of the play relates both to her attempt to disguise her age, and more important to the images connected with her young husband.

F.

We now find out why the Varsouviana music has been playing as background music. This was the song which played while Blanche and her young husband were dancing, and the same song, running through her mind is interrupted by the sound of her husband's gunshot. So now when Blanche hears the music, she must drink until she hears the gunshot which signals the end of the song.

G.

Centrally, this scene reveals both Blanche and Mitch to be very lonesome people who could possibly find happiness with each other. Each could fill some type of vacancy for the other. Thus the scene ends on a note of hope for both characters.

## SCENE SEVEN

*Summary*

A few weeks later, Stanley comes home to find that Blanche is soaking in a hot tub, even though it is blistering hot outside. It is Blanche's birthday and Stella has prepared a small party. Stanley makes Stella stop working and listen to him. He has found out something about Blanche. While Blanche is singing "It's Only a Paper Moon," Stanley reveals that Blanche has a notorious reputation in Laurel. She was so wild that the low class Flamingo Hotel asked her to move out. The army camp close by referred to Blanche as "out-of-bounds" and she was kicked out of her job for being mixed up with a seventeen-year-old boy. Blanche interrupts the conversation by calling for a towel. She notices a strange expression on Stella's face, but Stella assures her that all is well. Stella returns to Stanley and tries to explain that Blanche's early life was fraught with tragedy due to the young boy she had married and that Blanche was never able to recover completely. Stanley isn't interested in such "old history"; he is concerned only with the present.

When Stanley notices the birthday cake, he wonders if company is expected. Stella tells him that Mitch is invited over. Stanley explains that Mitch won't be there tonight because Mitch is an old friend of his and he had to tell Mitch everything that he had found out about Blanche. Stella is shocked and cries out that Blanche thought Mitch was going to marry her. Stanley corrects her by informing her that Mitch is not necessarily *through* with Blanche but he certainly *isn't* going to marry her. He also says that he has bought Blanche a bus ticket for next Tuesday and that she has to leave them. Stella protests, but Stanley is firm. He thinks that Blanche's future is "mapped out for her." He then screams for Blanche to come out of the bathroom so he can get in. When Blanche emerges, she notices that something has happened and is frightened.

*Commentary*

A.

As Blanche is in the bathroom bathing and singing about the

paper moon and make-believe world, the realistic Stanley comes home with a complete case against Blanche. He has collected all the facts and has assembled a list of all the lies that she has told him. Stanley is now ready for his final confrontation with Blanche. He now has all the information he needs to prove again his superiority over her.

B.

Stanley's actions, it must be remembered, stem from several motivations. Most important, Blanche has represented a threat to his marriage. His marital life has not been the same since the arrival of Blanche, and Stanley feels this. Secondly, he is tired of being referred to as vulgar and common. Even if he is vulgar, he feels that his life cannot hold a candle to the type of life Blanche has been leading. Thus he will reëstablish his own sense of importance only by proving how degenerate Blanche actually is. Lastly, Stanley is a person who cannot tolerate illusion or make-believe. He is the realist and must have "his cards on the table." Thus, he must, according to his nature, destroy all the illusions Blanche has been creating.

C.

Stanley does not have the sensibility to realize that perhaps Blanche and Mitch could have had a successful marriage in spite of Blanche's past. Instead, he feels some manly obligation to inform Mitch of Blanche's past life. And not only does he tell Mitch, but he buys a bus ticket for Blanche back to Laurel. Note that he could have bought a ticket to another town, but he cruelly buys one that sends her back to the scene of her last failure and the one place where she cannot possibly return.

D.

It is ironic that Blanche is bathing (again symbolic of a cleansing ritual) while all the past that she is trying to wash away is about to be revealed by Stanley.

## SCENE EIGHT

*Summary*

A short time later that evening, Blanche, Stella, and Stanley are finishing with Blanche's birthday party. She cannot understand why Mitch has not shown up. She tries to tell a joke, but no one laughs. Stella says that Stanley is "too busy making a pig of himself" and tells him to go wash and help her clear the table. Stanley explodes in anger, throws his plate to the floor, and warns Stella never to use such words to him again, that he is "king around here." As he leaves, Blanche demands to know what has happened. She plans on calling Mitch, but Stella asks her not to. She calls anyway, but Mitch is not at home. Stella prepares to light the birthday candles, while Stanley is complaining about the steam from the bath. The phone rings and when Stanley returns from answering it, he tells Blanche that he has a birthday gift for her. She is surprised and happy until she opens it and sees the bus ticket back to Laurel on Tuesday's bus. The polka music begins to play as Blanche is unable to do anything except flee from the room.

Stella doesn't understand why Stanley treated Blanche so brutally, especially since Blanche is so tender and delicate. In the light of Blanche's past experiences, Stanley refuses to believe that she is very delicate. Stella insists upon an explanation. Stanley reminds her that he was common when they first met and she loved it, especially at nights. And he tells Stella that they will be happy again after Blanche leaves. Suddenly Stella tells Stanley to take her to the hospital.

*Commentary*

A.

Scene Eight is the scene of violence. It begins with a small birthday party for Blanche, but as Blanche waits for Mitch to arrive, Stanley and Stella know that he is not coming. Thus there is a tension in the air which explodes when Stella tells Stanley that he is making a pig of himself and that he should wash and help her clear the table. Stanley violently throws his dishes away and then announces that he is king here.

B.

In actuality, we see in this scene that Blanche's presence is actually destroying Stanley and Stella's marriage. This type of scene would probably never have occurred if Blanche had not moved in; therefore, Stanley *is* fighting for his marriage.

C.

Stanley receives his revenge in full measure when he presents the return ticket to Blanche. The Varsouviana music begins again when Blanche sees the ticket. The music reinforces her predicament here, and the audience realizes that she is now on the verge of being trapped in a situation which will equal the death of her young husband.

D.

According to Stella, whom we must believe, Blanche was once "tender and trusting" but people abused her. Thus perhaps she has always been the type who was unfit for the world of reality.

E.

Stanley's last remarks make it apparent that before the arrival of Blanche, things were going fine between them. We see here that part of his revenge stems from the fact that Blanche has called him dirty, a pig, ape, and similar names.

## SCENE NINE

### *Summary*

Later that evening, Blanche is alone in the apartment. The doorbell startles her. It is Mitch who is still dressed in his working clothes and who is unshaven. Blanche pretends surprise but says she is glad to see him because he has stopped the polka music that was spinning in her head. She looks for a drink to offer him, but he doesn't want any of Stanley's whiskey. Blanche knows that something is wrong, but she says she will not "cross-examine" the witness. Mitch keeps trying to say something, but Blanche continues babbling. When Blanche offers him some liquor, he tells her that Stanley told him that she had been lapping it up all summer. He then says it is dark and wonders why Blanche has never gone out with him in the daytime. Mitch wants to turn on the lights, but Blanche pleads with him not to. She doesn't want light and truth; she wants magic and illusion. But Mitch jerks the lantern off the light and forces Blanche under it. He notices that she is older than he had supposed, but he could have accepted that if she had been straight.

He tells Blanche about the stories he has heard and how he checked them out and three people swore to them. When Mitch mentions the Flamingo, Blanche drops her pose and tells how after the death of her young husband, there was nothing to fill the void except intimacies with strangers. She went from one stranger to another until she had an affair with a seventeen-year-old boy. She was desperate when she came to New Orleans. Then she met Mitch, who told her that he needed someone and she needed someone. Mitch accuses her of lying to him. She says that she never lied in her heart. At this time, a street vendor passes by selling flowers for the dead. When Blanche hears the vendor, she thinks of all the deaths she has had to suffer, and that the opposite of death is desire. She even tells Mitch about her escapades with the Army camp which was near her house. Suddenly, Mitch puts his arms around her and demands what he has been missing all summer. She requests marriage. Mitch tells her she is not good enough. Blanche orders him to leave or she will start screaming. As he remains staring, she runs to the window and begins to scream *Fire*, wildly. Mitch stumbles out.

***Commentary***

A.

Note the opening description of Blanche. She is in her old dilapidated clothes—her last remnants of a past life. The "Varsouviana" music—the tune which played when her husband shot himself—is heard as background music and Blanche is drinking to escape it all.

B.

The appearance of Mitch, unshaven and dressed in his dirty work clothes emphasizes again that he is Blanche's last chance—that he is a rough and rather uncouth character.

C.

With Mitch's appearance, Blanche immediately begins to act the part of the innocent young girl and the polka music stops. But almost immediately she realizes that something is wrong and the music begins again. During the first part of this scene, Blanche talks so much that Mitch doesn't have a chance to make his accusations against her. Her incessant line of chatter functions to cover up her fears and to postpone hearing what she fears to hear.

D.

Mitch's first confrontation comes when he forces Blanche under the light. This act has multiple significance. First, on the realistic level, Blanche has deceived Mitch about her age and the light reveals Blanche's deception. The revelation of this deception leads to the other deceptions. Secondly, Blanche has constantly avoided the light ever since her young husband shot himself. She has had nothing stronger than a candle light since his death. Thus, Blanche has passed her life in semi-darkness and to be forced into the light makes her violate her inner nature. Third, being forced into the light here symbolizes the revelation of the truth about Blanche's past life. She has tried to conceal her life of dissipation and when Mitch forces her under the light, it is the same as making her realize and confess her past life. And fourth, Blanche's whole theory of living involves magic and illusion. She doesn't want realism. Instead, she prefers the magic of illusion. And rather than the truth, she lives for "what *ought* to be." Thus forcing Blanche into the light makes her see things in their ugly realism – that is, it makes her see how her life actually was instead of how it *ought to have been*.

E.

Blanche's confession of her past life is almost too much. It has that Tennessee Williams quality of sensationalism. It is almost unbelievable, and as some critics would maintain, unnecessary for her to have such a lurid and degenerate past. Her confession doesn't seem to fit with this delicate moth-like creature on the edge of disintegration. But the opposite argument must be seen. Williams has attempted to show how Blanche's over-delicate and over-sensitive nature was the reason she sought escape from her failure with her young husband by turning to alcohol and to intimacies with strangers.

F.

When Mitch accuses Blanche of lying to him, she maintains that she never lied "inside. I didn't lie in my heart." Blanche means that she has used some deception to trap Mitch, but a certain amount of illusion is a woman's charm, but as she said to Stanley in Scene Two, "when a thing is important, I tell the truth." And she did tell the truth to Mitch when she told him that she loved and needed him and that they needed each other.

G.

Mitch, having learned of Blanche's past, then feels that she should sleep with him. In his disappointment with the truth about Blanche, he doesn't realize that she could give herself to a stranger but not freely to someone whom she knew as well as she knows Mitch and certainly not under such crude circumstances. Therefore, at the end of the scene, Blanche is at her lowest ebb of existence now that Stanley has given her a bus ticket back to Laurel and Mitch has deserted her.

## SCENE TEN

### *Summary*

Later that evening, Blanche is dressed in an old faded gown and has a rhinestone tiara on her head. She has been drinking heavily. She is talking to herself when Stanley enters. He tells her that the baby won't come before morning, and the doctors sent him home. He wonders about the outfit that Blanche has on. She tells him a fabulous story about how she just received an invitation for a cruise in the Caribbean with a Mr. Shep Huntleigh. Stanley drinks some beer and gets out the silk pajamas which he wore on his wedding night. Blanche thinks how wonderful it will be to have some privacy again and to be among something other than swine. Blanche tells Stanley how Mitch came to her imploring her forgiveness, but she sent him away because "deliberate cruelty is not forgivable." Then Stanley attacks her, telling her she is lying and that she has no invitation. Blanche flees to the telephone trying to reach Shep Huntleigh, but she can't seem to compose a message. She leaves the phone to get the address. Stanley replaces the phone on the hook. Blanche wants him to stand aside so she can pass, and Stanley thinks that it might not be too bad to interfere with her. As he advances toward her, Blanche breaks a bottle so as "to twist the broken end in your face." He springs on her as she sinks to the floor. He picks up her inert body and carries it into the bedroom.

*Commentary*

A.

This scene presents the final confrontation between Blanche and Stanley, with Stanley emerging as the undisputed winner.

B.

The beginning of the scene reëstablishes the basic difference between Blanche and Stanley. She is once again living in her world of illusion and pretense—a world that Stanley, the realist, cannot understand or tolerate.

C.

Blanche says that she dismissed Mitch, because "deliberate cruelty is not forgivable. It is the one unforgivable thing in my opinion." Therefore since Blanche was once deliberately cruel to her young husband, she has since formulated this idea. And of course, she must view herself as being unforgivable for her cruelty to him. This perhaps motivates a lot of her actions, but her statement comes at an ironic point—that is, just before Stanley is about to rape her—an act of extreme cruelty.

D.

In his exhilaration over the forthcoming birth of his child, Stanley is seen as a wild animal on the prey. For the first time, he sees Blanche as someone whom it "wouldn't be bad to—interfere with..." This idea plants the idea of seduction in his mind. He also feels that Blanche has been "swilling down my liquor" all summer and that he deserves a little pay. But also, Stanley cannot understand why a woman who has slept with so many men would object to sleeping with him. And most important, Stanley has always functioned with the idea of enjoying the things that are *his*—that is, "his car, his radio, everything that is his, that bears his emblem of the gaudy seed-bearer." Blanche has lived in his house, has eaten his food, and has drunk his liquor, but she is definitely not his; in fact, she is openly antagonistic toward him. Thus, his rape is partially to prove again his superiority over her. And since her presence in his house has almost destroyed his marriage, he feels no remorse or regret over Blanche's destruction.

E.

Blanche's horrified aversion to sleeping with Stanley is not based on any moral grounds. Instead, he represents every aspect of life which she is unable to cope with. He appears to her as her destroyer, and his rape of her is actually the cause of her madness. And she was not strong enough to defend herself against this hostile force. Thus it is not the actual rape which causes her madness, but the idea that she was raped by a man who represents everything unacceptable to her. Thus, she is symbolically unable to cope with the brutal realistic world represented by Stanley.

## SCENE ELEVEN

***Summary***

Several weeks later, Stella is seen packing some of Blanche's things. There is another poker party going on. This time, Stanley is winning. Eunice comes in to help with the packing. Stella wonders if she is doing the right thing by sending Blanche to the state institution. Stella tells Eunice that she couldn't continue to live with Stanley if she believed Blanche's story. Eunice assures Stella that she is doing the only sensible thing. Blanche comes from the bathroom, and she possesses a "hysterical vivacity." She wonders if she has received a call. Blanche speaks suddenly with a hysteria demanding to know what is going on. She feels trapped and wants to get out of the trap. Stella and Eunice help her get dressed. Blanche eats some unwashed grapes and thinks that she would like to die somewhere on the sea from eating unwashed grapes and be buried in a clean white sack.

The doctor and a matron from the state institution arrive to pick up Blanche. Eunice announces that "someone is calling for Blanche." Blanche is ready to go but doesn't want to pass through the room where the men are playing poker. When she sees the doctor, she panics and tries to run. Stanley blocks her way, and along with the matron, advances toward her. Stanley assures her that she left nothing here but the paper lantern which he tears off the light bulb and hands to Blanche. As Blanche screams and tries to break away, Stella runs out on the porch where Eunice tries to comfort her. Meanwhile, the matron pins Blanche down. The doctor advances and speaks quietly and softly to Blanche. She responds to his quietness and says that she has "always depended on the kindness of strangers." The doctor leads her out and Stanley comes to comfort Stella by fondling her breasts.

*Commentary*

A.

This scene balances with the poker game in Scene Three. But where Stanley was losing in the earlier game, he is now the winner, suggesting that he is once again the undisputed master in his own house.

B.

Williams' position is probably best stated in Eunice's remark to Stella after Stella says that she couldn't go on living with Stanley if Blanche's story is true. Eunice tells her "Don't ever believe it. Life has got to go on. No matter what happens, you've got to keep on going." But apparently Blanche did not have the strength to go on living in spite of everything. She was too delicate to be able to withstand the pressures of living in a brutal realistic world.

C.

When Blanche refuses to go with the doctor and matron, she tells them that she has forgotten something. It is then that Stanley wonders what and takes off the "magic" Chinese lantern from the light leaving the naked light bulb glaring at Blanche. This is the final blow for Blanche who tries to escape and is trapped by the matron. Again the light symbolism emphasizes Blanche's desire to live in a world of semi-illusion which contradicts Stanley's world.

D.

The play ends with Stanley's comforting Stella in the only way he knows how—that is, by unbuttoning her blouse and fondling her breasts, again emphasizing him as the "gaudy seed-bearer."

E.

The last line of the play puns on the man's world as Steve announces that the game is "seven-card stud," a particularly wild poker game.

# CHARACTER ANALYSES

## BLANCHE DUBOIS

Blanche DuBois appears in the first scene dressed in white, the symbol of purity and innocence. She is seen as a moth-like creature. She is delicate, refined, and sensitive. She is cultured and intelligent. She can't stand a vulgar remark or a vulgar action. She would never willingly hurt someone. She doesn't want realism; she prefers magic. She doesn't always tell the truth, but she tells "what ought to be truth." Yet she has lived a life that would make the most degenerate person seem timid. She is, in general, one of Williams' characters who do not belong in this world. And her type will always be at the mercy of the brutal, realistic world.

Early in her life, Blanche had married a young boy who had a softness and tenderness "which wasn't like a man's," even though he "wasn't the least bit effeminate looking." By unexpectedly entering a room, she found him in a compromising situation with an older man. They went that night to a dance where a polka was playing. In the middle of the dance, Blanche told her young husband that he disgusted her. This deliberate act of cruelty on Blanche's part caused her young husband to commit suicide. Earlier, her love had been like a "blinding light," and since that night Blanche has never had any light stronger than a dim candle. Blanche has always thought she failed her young lover when he most needed her. She felt also that she was cruel to him in a way that Stanley would like to be cruel to her. And Blanche's entire life has been affected by this early tragic event.

Immediately following this event, Blanche was subjected to a series of deaths in her family and the ultimate loss of the ancestral home. The deaths were ugly, slow, and tortuous. They illustrated the ugliness and brutality of life.

To escape from these brutalities and to escape from the lonely void created by her young husband's death, Blanche turned to alcohol and sexual promiscuity. The alcohol helped her to forget. When troubled, the dance tune that was playing when Allan committed suicide haunts her until she drinks enough so as to hear the shot which then signals the end of the music.

Blanche gives herself to men for other reasons. She feels that she had failed her young husband in some way. Therefore, she tries to alleviate her guilt by giving herself at random to other young men. And by sleeping with others, she is trying to fill the void left by Allan's death—"intimacies with strangers was all I seemed able to fill my empty heart with." And she was particularly drawn to very young men who would remind her of her young husband. During these years of promiscuity, Blanche has never been able to find anyone to fill the emptiness. Thus Blanche's imagined failure to her young husband and her constant encounter with the ugliness of death forced the delicate young girl to seek distraction by and forgetfulness through intimacies with strangers and through alcohol which could make the tune in her head stop.

But throughout all of these episodes, Blanche has still retained a degree of innocence and purity. She still plays the role of the ideal type of person she would like to be. She refuses to see herself as she is but instead creates the illusion of what *ought to be*. Thus, in her first encounters, she fails with Stanley, because she attempts to be what she thinks a lady *should* be rather than being frank, open, and honest as Stanley would have liked it.

Blanche's actions with Stanley are dictated by her basic nature. The woman must create an illusion. "After all, a woman's charm is fifty percent illusion." And if Blanche cannot function as a woman, then her life is invalid. She therefore tries to captivate Stanley by flirting with him and by using all of her womanly charms. She knows no other way to enter into her present surroundings. Likewise, she must change the apartment. She can't have the glaring open light bulb. She must have subdued light. She must live in the quiet half-lit world of charm and illusion. She does not want to see things clearly but wants all ugly truths covered over with the beauty of imagination and illusion.

But Blanche also realizes that she must attract men with her physical body. Thus, she does draw Mitch's attention by undressing in the light so that he can see the outline of her body.

When Blanche meets Mitch, she realizes that here is a strong harbor where she can rest. Here is the man who can give her a sense of belonging and who is also captivated by her girlish charms. She deceives him into thinking her prim and proper but in actuality, Blanche would like to *be* prim and proper. And as she later told Mitch, "inside, I never lied." Her essential nature and being have never been changed by her promiscuity. She gave of her body but not of her deeper self. To Mitch, she is ready to give her whole being.

Then Mitch forces her to admit her past life. With this revelation, Blanche is deprived of her chief attributes – that is, her illusions and her pretense. She is then forced to admit all of her past. After hearing her confessions, we see that Mitch aligns himself with the Stanley world. He cannot understand the reasons why Blanche had to give herself to so many people, and if she did, he thinks that she should have no objections to sleeping with one more man. But Blanche's intimacies have always been with strangers. She cannot wantonly give herself to someone for whom she has an affection. Thus she forces Mitch to leave.

Later that same night when Stanley comes from the hospital, Blanche encounters the same type of brutality. Stanley rapes Blanche, assuming that she has slept with so many men in the past one more would not matter. In actuality, Blanche's action in the first part of the play indicates that on first acquaintance, when Stanley was a stranger, she desired him or at least flirted with him. But Stanley was never able to understand the sensitivity behind Blanche's pretense. Even when Stella refers to Blanche as delicate, Stanley cries out in disbelief "Some delicate piece she is." It is, then, Stanley's forced brutality which causes Blanche to crack up. The rape is Blanche's destruction as an individual. In all previous sexual encounters, Blanche had freely given of herself. But to be taken so cruelly and so brutally by a man who represents all qualities which Blanche found obnoxious caused her entire world to collapse.

Blanche's last remarks in the play seem to echo pathetically her plight and predicament in life. She goes with the doctor because he seems to be a gentleman and because he is a stranger. As she leaves, she says "I have always depended on the kindness of strangers." Thus, Blanche's life ends in the hands of the strange doctor. She was too delicate, too sensitive, too refined, and too beautiful to live in the realistic world. Her illusions had no place in the Kowalski world and when the illusions were destroyed, Blanche was also destroyed.

## STANLEY KOWALSKI

We cannot deny the fact that Stanley Kowalski is a fascinating character. The usual reaction is to see him as a brute because of the way that he treats the delicate Blanche. Some will even go so far as to dislike this man intensely. But this dislike would stem from too much identification with Blanche.

Stanley Kowalski lives in a basic, fundamental world which allows for no subtleties and no refinements. He is the man who likes to lay his cards on the table. He can understand no relationship between man and woman except a sexual one where he sees the man's role as giving and taking pleasure from this relationship. He possesses no quality that would not be considered manly in the most basic sense. By more sensitive people, he is seen as common, crude, and vulgar. Certainly, his frankness will allow for no deviation from the straightforward truth. His dress is loud and gaudy. He relishes in loud noises, and his voice rings out like a loud bellow.

To the over-sensitive person, such as Blanche, Stanley represents a holdover from the Stone Age. He is bestial and brutal and determined to destroy that which is not his. He is like the Stone Age savage bringing home the meat from the kill. He is animal-like and his actions are such. He eats like an animal and grunts his approval or disapproval. When aroused to anger, he strikes back by throwing things, like the radio. Or he breaks dishes or strikes his wife. He is the man of physical action.

Even the symbols connected with Stanley support his brutal, animal-like approach to life. In the first scene, he is seen bringing home the raw meat. His clothes are loud and gaudy. His language is rough and crude. His outside pleasures are bowling—a sport used symbolically to suggest the masculine phallic element of Stanley—and poker. When he is losing at poker, he is unpleasant and demanding. When he is winning, he is happy as a little boy.

He is, then, "the gaudy seed-bearer," who takes pleasure in his masculinity. "Animal joy in his being is implicit," and he enjoys mainly those things that are *his*—his wife, his apartment, his liquor, "his car, his radio, everything that is his, that bears his emblem of the gaudy seed-bearer."

With the appearance of Blanche, Stanley feels an uncomfortable threat to those things that are his. Blanche becomes a threat to his way of life; she is a foreign element, a hostile force, a superior being whom he can't understand. She is a challenge and a threat. He feels most strongly that she is a threat to his marriage. Thus when the basic man, such as Stanley, feels threatened, he must strike back. It is a survival of the fittest.

Stanley first feels the threat when he finds out that Belle Reve has been lost. He does not care for Belle Reve as a bit of ancestral property, but instead, he feels that a part of it is *his*. If his wife has been swindled, he has been swindled. He has lost property, something that belonged to him. He probes into the problem without tact or diplomacy. He goes straight to the truth without any shortcuts. His only concern is to discover whether he has been cheated. He does not concern himself with the feelings of Blanche. He wants only to force the issue to its completion.

Stanley feels the first threat to his marriage after the big fight he has with Stella after the poker game. He knows that this would not have occurred if Blanche had not been present. It is her presence which is causing the dissension between him and his wife. Then the following morning when he overhears himself being referred to as bestial, common, brutal, and a survivor of the Stone Age, he is justifiably enraged against Blanche. He resents her superior attitude and bides his time.

Throughout Blanche's stay at his house, he feels that she has drunk *his* liquor, eaten *his* food, used *his* house, but still has belittled him and has opposed him. She has never conceded to him his right to be the "king" in his own house. Thus, he must sit idly by and see his marriage and home destroyed, and himself belittled, or else he must strike back. His attack is slow and calculated. He begins to compile information about Blanche's past life. He must present her past life to his wife so that she can determine who is the superior person. When he has his information accumulated, he is convinced that however common he is, his life and his past is far superior to Blanche's. Now that he feels his superiority again, he begins to act. He feels that having proved how degenerate Blanche actually is, he is now justified in punishing her directly for all the indirect insults he has had to suffer from her. Thus he buys her the bus ticket back to Laurel and reveals her past to Mitch.

Consequently, when we approach the rape scene, we must understand that Blanche has made Stanley endure quite a bit. She has never been sympathetic toward him. She has ridiculed him. Earlier she had even flirted with him but she has never been his. Thus, when Stanley finds out that she has slept so indiscriminately with so many people, he cannot understand why she should object to one more. Thus, he rapes her partly out of revenge, partly because one more man shouldn't make any difference, and finally, so that she will be his in the only way he fully understands.

Stanley, then, is the hard brutal man who does not understand the refinements of life. He is controlled by natural instincts untouched by the advances of civilization. Thus, when something threatens him, he must strike back in order to preserve his own threatened existence. If someone gets destroyed, that is the price that must be paid. It is the survival of the fittest, and Stanley is the strongest.

## STELLA KOWALSKI

The glaring contrast and fierce struggle between the two worlds of Stanley Kowalski and Blanche DuBois are the main themes of Williams' play. These two worlds are so diametrically opposed that they can never meet. Thus, in order to bring these two together—to have these two encounter each other—Williams has created Stella. By simply having her married to Stanley and by having her be Blanche's sister, Williams then creates the perfect opportunity of bringing these two opposing worlds together under one roof.

Stella DuBois Kowalski is, then, a vital part in the struggle between these two worlds, and she is also the bridge between these two worlds. Both Blanche and Stanley are guilty of trying to involve Stella in their quarrel. Both attempt to win Stella over as an ally. Stella is the battlefield for those two warring factions, and both try to use her to accomplish their own ends. But Stella also seems to be the only answer to peace, for she is the only bridge between these two apparent opposites. She comes from Blanche's refined, educated, and sensitive world. She has, therefore, attained a mixture either consciously or unconsciously.

It is apparent that Stella is a battleground for the DuBois-Kowalski feud. Blanche continually tries to turn Stella away from Stanley, by belittling him every chance she has. She tries to prevent her sister from returning to her husband after Stella had been beaten by Stanley during the card game. Blanche does not try to hide her opinion of Stanley when she decides to tell Stella of her true feelings for her brother-in-law. She calls Stanley "common," "bestial," and "sub-human." Stella seems to become the tangible symbol of victory between the two warring parties. Blanche does her best in trying to grasp this symbol for herself. Blanche's influence is definitely weighty. The argument between Stanley and his wife in Scene Three is directly caused by Blanche's insistence on playing the radio. Stella shows strong signs of her sister's influence. She even seems to repeat exactly what Blanche would say, "drunk—drunk—animal thing, you!" In another instance, she says, "Mr. Kowalski is too busy making a pig of himself to think of anything else!" These are words that most likely would come from Blanche's own mouth and Stella would never have uttered them before Blanche's arrival. Thus, Blanche has had some influence upon Stella.

But Blanche is not alone in her hopes to win over Stella, for Stanley is also guilty of trying to mold his wife's mind. He is continually trying to convince Stella that they had a better life together before her sister's arrival. He wants Stella to ask her sister to leave, and he continues his efforts in doing this. He does not need Stella's consent to throw Blanche out of his house but he, nevertheless, strives to get his wife's approval. Stella is reminded of the "colored lights" of their sex life together and of the happiness they once shared. He delights in telling Stella of her sister's immorality, hoping that this too will turn his wife against Blanche. Stanley tells her that it will be all right once again between them as soon as Blanche leaves.

But Stella's function is not just to be an object in this struggle, to be merely swayed from one side to the other. She also seems to be the only hope of a compromise between these two different backgrounds. As Blanche and Stanley represent two diametrically opposed worlds, so Stella represents a bridge between the two poles. For Stella shows that a meeting point of coexistence is possible between Blanche's and Stanley's separate worlds. Stella still has many qualities of Belle Reve. She has not allowed a gentle and refined nature to completely disappear simply because she has accepted Stanley and all he stands for. Nor has she allowed her upbringing to stand in the way of enjoying life with her raw and lusty husband. She has rather combined both worlds into one and has shown that these two apparent opposites are, if not compatible, at least coexistable. The problem between the play's two main characters seems not to be the irreconcilable worlds which they represent, but the rigid inflexibility of Stanley and Blanche in their respective attitudes. Stella seems to indicate that such a reconciliation is possible. She is not a perfect blend; however, she does show that a mixture of the two viewpoints can be workable.

But one should not maintain the position that Stella is a strong character. She is far from this. Blanche appears to be the weaker of the two sisters but this is a false impression. If Stella were a strong character with a definite mind of her own, a three-way conflict and not a two-way conflict would appear in the play. Stella would have a definite standard of action and would pursue this throughout the course of the play. But her definite vacillation between the two opposite poles of Blanche and Stanley is only possible because of her weakness. This quality in her character enables her to become a pawn in the death struggle between the two major characters. This weakness alone makes her a battleground. Stella does not attain the blend of the two worlds because she wills it; they simply come together to form this blend without her assistance. She remains passive throughout the play.

Thus, the character of Stella fulfills two basic functions. She is deeply involved in the battle between her sister and her husband. She is torn between the two factions unmercifully. But she is also the only one who can attempt to bridge the gap between these two arch enemies and all that they represent. She certainly does have some thoughts independent of the dynamic forces in her home; however, on the whole, she maintains a passive role.

## HAROLD MITCHELL (MITCH)

Harold Mitchell is first seen as one of the four poker players in the third scene. The players speak coarsely, enjoying primitive, direct humor, mixing it with the cards, chips, and whiskey—that is, all except Mitch. He seems to be somewhat different. He is first distinguished from the other three when he is teased about his concern for his mother. He excuses this soft-heartedness by explaining that she is ill and unable to sleep until he comes in at night. In disdain, the hot-tempered Stanley tells him to go home. A few lines later, a second aspect of Mitch is revealed as he meets Blanche DuBois. His awkward courtesy and embarrassment show a consciousness of manners seldom seen in that raffish section of New Orleans. Blanche is quick to notice the hint of sensitivity in him that makes him seem superior to the others. Although he carries a silver cigarette case engraved with a quote from a sonnet, his words describing the romance and sorrow that inspired it seem trite and inadequate. At this point, Blanche provides the imagination and sympathy, while Mitch answers with his characteristically sincere commonplaces. His sensitivity appears rather clumsy in comparison, but he does half apologize saying that Stanley and his friends must strike Blanche as a pretty rough bunch. Mitch's awkward imitation of the romantic gestures of Blanche is shown in the stage direction of this scene. He is a "dancing bear" following the steps of her waltz. But this first appearance *does* characterize Mitch as the most sensitive member of the Kowalski world.

Mitch's limitations become more and more apparent as the play progresses, especially as Blanche believes she has found in him the kindness she so desperately needs. He is the representative of the decent gentleman who could save Blanche from the past from which she is trying to flee. However, we must remember that it is only in the rough society of men like Stanley that Mitch can be considered a valuable discovery. Blanche would be more aware of the differences in education and temperament if she were not in such immediate danger of breaking down emotionally. In the sixth scene, as they return from an evening at the amusement park, one sees the disparity in their intellects. Mitch only dimly feels that Blanche is laughing at him as he says he has never met anyone like her. She has succeeded in presenting a convincing image of innocence and sincerity; he accepts the appearance in tolerant good nature. The respect he affords her in not attempting to make love to her again separates him from Stanley. There is a contrast between his proud discussion of his physique and his mild request that Blanche can "just give him a slap" when he steps out of bounds. One is impressed by the wide gap of perception between him and Blanche. She is playing a role with demureness and delicate deceit while Mitch talks of himself in the bragging fashion of a young boy.

As soon as Mitch mentions his mother, Blanche draws him to the subject of love, seeing in him a warmth and "capacity for devotion." She tells him at last the story of her early marriage, in which lies the source of her torment. Mitch again responds awkwardly but is deeply moved. His sympathy and momentary understanding are sincere. At that point, he is at his highest in the play, although brought there by the influence of Blanche. It is in the denouement that he is again won over by the power of the world of Stanley, but for a brief moment Mitch had the possibility of saving the fragile Blanche and of being redeemed by her. The very characteristics that make him ordinary would have been indispensable to her—his honesty, stability, loyalty, and love. It is consistent with his lack of imagination that he should leave Blanche when confronted with her past. He could not see through her acting during the summer, for she herself had come to believe in her role. Her world where truth and fiction are blended was incomprehensible to him. Mitch failed to understand that Blanche could sincerely tell him, "Never inside, I didn't lie in my heart." His world crumbled, and he was unable to perceive the actual depth of Blanche's feelings.

In the last scene Mitch is once again playing poker, moody and ill-tempered. He bursts out at Stanley angrily, betraying his uneasiness. He is unable to concentrate on the game when he hears Blanche's voice, although several weeks have passed since their previous meeting. By staring down at his hands on the table, he is able to maintain the control he loses a few minutes later. Alone in his sympathy for Blanche, especially as he understands her aversion to this destructive environment, he lashes out wildly at Stanley. He seems to blame Stanley for interfering with a relationship that should have been left alone, but then he collapses in ineffectual sobs. Mitch fails by realizing too late the vulnerable beauty of Blanche and thus, he is left as lonely and alone as is Blanche.

## QUESTIONS

1. Why does Blanche avoid strong light? (See discussion of structure and the commentaries after Scenes One, Six, and Nine.)

2. How are specific physical symbols used to characterize the essential nature of Stanley Kowalski? (See commentaries A and B after Scene One, and the character analysis of Stanley.)

3. How is it possible that two such opposite people as Blanche and Stanley could possibly meet? (See commentary after Scene One and the character analysis of Stella.)

4. Why does Blanche so openly flirt with Stanley in the first part of the play? What significance does this later have? (See commentary B of Scene Two and the character analyses of Blanche and Stanley.)

5. What is the purpose of the two poker games? (See commentaries after Scenes Three and Eleven.)

6. What do Blanche's actions with the young newspaper boy indicate about her conflict? (See commentary C after Scene Five and the character analysis of Blanche.)

7. Characterize the essential differences between the Kowalski and the DuBois worlds. (See section on structure.)

8. How do Blanche's many baths influence the action of the drama? (See commentary A after Scene Two and commentary D after Scene Seven.)

9. What implications are there in Mitch's act of forcing Blanche under the naked light bulb? (See commentary D after Scene Nine and the character analysis of Blanche.)

10. Why does Blanche's rape totally destroy her? (See commentary E after Scene Ten and the character analysis of Blanche.)

11. Justify Stanley's antagonism toward Blanche. (See character analysis of Stanley.)

12. Using evidence from the play, try to determine which is the real Blanche, the innocent and charming Blanche or the degenerate and promiscuous Blanche. (See commentaries after Scene Five and the character analysis of Blanche and the section on structure.)

## SUGGESTED THEME TOPICS

1. Show how each subsequent meeting between Blanche and Stanley increases in violence and antagonism.

2. Justify the Kowalski world as being superior to the DuBois world.

3. In spite of Blanche's past life, her deceit, and her artificialty, most readers and viewers tend to sympathize with and align themselves with her. How can this emotional reaction (or attachment) toward Blanche be justified?

4. Describe how Stella's child offers the only hope of a reconciliation between the two opposing worlds of Kowalski and DuBois.

5. Show how a Mitch-Blanche marriage could have been a perfect marriage if Stanley had not interfered.

6. Where do you consider Williams' final view toward illusion and reality to lie? Does he align himself with Stanley's reality and brutal honesty, or with Blanche's illusion and pretense?

## SELECTED BIBLIOGRAPHY

### GENERAL

DONAHUE, FRANCIS. *The Dramatic World of Tennessee Williams.* New York: Frederick Ungar, 1964.

FALK, SIGNI LENEA. *Tennessee Williams.* 2nd ed. Boston: Twayne, 1978.

HAYMAN, RONALD. *Tennessee Williams: Everyone Else Is an Audience.* New Haven, Connecticut: Yale University Press, 1993.

RASKY, HARRY. *Tennessee Williams: A Portrait in Laughter and Lamentation.* New York: Dodd, Mead, 1986.

STANTON, STEPHEN S. *Tennessee Williams: A Collection of Critical Essays.* Englewood Cliffs, New Jersey: Prentice-Hall, 1977.

WILLIAMS, DAKIN, and SHEPHERD MEAD. *Tennessee Williams: An Intimate Portrait.* New York: Arbor House, 1983.

## *THE GLASS MENAGERIE*

BAK, JOHN S. "'Celebrate Her with Strings': Leitmotifs and the Multifaceted 'Strings' in Williams's *The Glass Menagerie.*" *Notes on Mississippi Writers* 24 (1992): 81–87.

BALACHANDRAN, K. "Marriage and Family Life in Tennessee Williams." *Notes on Mississippi Writers* 21 (1989): 69–76.

BLOOM, HAROLD, ed. *Tennessee Williams's* The Glass Menagerie. New York: Chelsea, 1988.

JONES, JOHN H. "The Missing Link: The Father in *The Glass Menagerie.*" *Notes on Mississippi Writers* 20 (1988): 29–38.

KING, THOMAS L. "Irony and Distance in *The Glass Menagerie.*" *Educational Theatre Journal* 25 (1973): 207–14.

KOLIN, PHILIP C. "Black and Multi-Racial Productions of Tennessee Williams's *The Glass Menagerie.*" *Journal of Dramatic Theory and Criticism* 9 (1995): 96–128.

LEVY, ERIC P. "'Through Soundproof Glass': The Prison of Self-Consciousness in *The Glass Menagerie.*" *Modern Drama* 36 (1993): 529–37.

LILLY, MARK. "Tennessee Williams: *The Glass Menagerie* and *A Streetcar Named Desire.*" *Lesbian and Gay Writing: An Anthology of Critical Essays*. Ed. Mark Lilly. Philadelphia: Temple University Press, 1990. 153–63.

PARKER, BRIAN. "The Composition of *The Glass Menagerie*: An Argument for Complexity." *Modern Drama* 25 (1982): 409–22.

PARKER, R. B. "The Circle Closed: A Psychological Reading of *The Glass Menagerie* and *The Two Character Play.*" *Modern Drama* 28 (1985): 517–34.

__________, ed. The Glass Menagerie: *A Collection of Critical Essays*. Englewood Cliffs, New Jersey: Prentice-Hall, 1983.

POTTER, ALEX. "*The Glass Menagerie* by Tennessee Williams." *CRUX* 14 (1980): 20–26.

REYNOLDS, JAMES. "The Failure of Technology in *The Glass Menagerie*." *Modern Drama* 34 (1991): 522–27.

SAROTTE, GEORGES MICHEL. "Fluidity and Differentiation in Three Plays by Tennessee Williams: *The Glass Menagerie*, *A Streetcar Named Desire*, and *Cat on a Hot Tin Roof*." *Staging Difference: Cultural Pluralism in American Theatre and Drama*. Ed. Marc Maufort. New York: Peter Lang, 1995. 141–56.

SHEEHY, CATHERINE. "Flexi-Glass: Tennessee Williams's Supremely Malleable Menagerie." *Theater* 22 (1990–1991): 79–82.

SMITH, WILLIAM JAY. "The Making of *The Glass Menagerie*." *The New Criterion* 14 (1996): 72–77.

STEIN, ROGER B. "*The Glass Menagerie* Revisited: Catastrophe Without Violence." *Tennessee Williams: A Collection of Critical Essays*. Ed. Stephen S. Stanton. Englewood Cliffs, New Jersey: Prentice-Hall, 1977. 36–44.

USUI, MASAMI. "'A World of Her Own' in Tennessee Williams's *The Glass Menagerie*." *Studies in Culture and the Humanities* 1 (1992): 21–37.

VAN LAAN, THOMAS F. "'Shut Up!' 'Be Quiet!' 'Hush!': Talk and Its Suppression in Three Plays by Tennessee Williams." *Comparative Drama* 22 (1988): 244–65.

### *A STREETCAR NAMED DESIRE*

ADLER, THOMAS P. A Streetcar Named Desire: *The Moth and the Lantern*. Boston: Twayne, 1990.

BLOOM, HAROLD, ed. *Tennessee Williams's* A Streetcar Named Desire. New York: Chelsea, 1988.

CAHIR, LINDA COSTANZO. "The Artful Rerouting of *A Streetcar Named Desire.*" *Literature Film Quarterly* 22 (1994): 72–77.

CARDULLO, BERT. "The Meaning of 'Belle Reve' in *A Streetcar Named Desire.*" *Language Quarterly* 32 (1994): 220–22.

FLECHE, ANNE. "The Space of Madness and Desire: Tennessee Williams and *Streetcar.*" *Modern Drama* 38 (1995): 496–509.

GRONBECK-TEDESCO, JOHN L. "Absence and the Actor's Body: Marlon Brando's Performance in *A Streetcar Named Desire* on Stage and in Film." *Studies in American Drama* 8 (1993): 115–26.

HANKS, PAMELA ANNE. "Must We Acknowledge What We Mean? The Viewer's Role in Filmed Versions of *A Streetcar Named Desire.*" *Journal of Popular Film and Television* 14 (1986): 114–22.

HULLEY, KATHLEEN. "The Fate of the Symbolic in *A Streetcar Named Desire.*" *Drama and Symbolism.* Ed. James Redmond. New York: Cambridge University Press, 1982. 89–99.

KAILO, KAARINA. "Blanche Dubois and Salome as New Women: Old Lunatics in Modern Drama." *Madness in Drama.* Ed. James Redmond. New York: Cambridge University Press, 1993. 119–36.

KOLIN, PHILIP C. "*A Streetcar Named Desire*: A Playwrights' Forum." *Michigan Quarterly Review* 29 (1990): 173–203.

__________. *Confronting Tennessee Williams's* A Streetcar Named Desire*: Essays in Cultural Pluralism.* Westport, Connecticut: Greenwood Press, 1993.

__________. "The First Critical Assessment of *A Streetcar Named Desire*: The Streetcar Tryouts and the Reviewers." *Journal of Dramatic Theory and Criticism* 6 (1991): 45–67.

LANT, KATHLEEN MARGARET. "A Streetcar Named Misogyny." *Violence in Drama*. Ed. James Redmond. New York: Cambridge University Press, 1991. 225–38.

LILLY, MARK. "Tennessee Williams: *The Glass Menagerie* and *A Streetcar Named Desire*." *Lesbian and Gay Writing: An Anthology of Critical Essays*. Ed. Mark Lilly. Philadelphia: Temple University Press, 1990. 153–63.

MILLER, JORDAN Y. *Twentieth Century Interpretations of* A Streetcar Named Desire. Englewood Cliffs, New Jersey: Prentice-Hall, 1971.

SAROTTE, GEORGES MICHEL. "Fluidity and Differentiation in Three Plays by Tennessee Williams: *The Glass Menagerie*, *A Streetcar Named Desire*, and *Cat on a Hot Tin Roof*." *Staging Difference: Cultural Pluralism in American Theatre and Drama*. Ed. Marc Maufort. New York: Peter Lang, 1995. 141–56.

VLASOPOLOS, ANCA. "Authorizing History: Victimization in *A Streetcar Named Desire*." *Feminist Rereadings of Modern American Drama*. Ed. June Schlueter. Rutherford, New Jersey: Fairleigh Dickinson University Press, 1989. 149–70.

WILHELMI, NANCY O. "The Language of Power and Powerlessness: Verbal Combat in the Plays of Tennessee Williams." *The Text & Beyond: Essays in Literary Linguistics*. Ed. Cynthia Goldin Bernstein. Tuscaloosa: University of Alabama Press, 1994. 217–26.

# NOTES

# NOTES

# NOTES

# NOTES

# NOTES

# NOTES

# NOTES